IT HAPPENED TO ME

Series Editor: Arlene Hirschfelder

Books in the It Happened To Me series are designed for inquisitive teens digging for answers about certain illnesses, social issues, or lifestyle interests. Whether you are deep into your teen years or just entering them, these books are gold mines of up-to-date information, riveting teen views, and great visuals to help you figure out stuff. Besides special boxes highlighting singular facts, each book is enhanced with the latest reading list, websites, and an index. Perfect for browsing, there's loads of expert information by acclaimed writers to help parents, guardians, and librarians understand teen illness, tough situations, and lifestyle choices.

1. *Learning Disabilities: The Ultimate Teen Guide,* by Penny Hutchins Paquette and Cheryl Gerson Tuttle, 2003.
2. *Epilepsy: The Ultimate Teen Guide,* by Kathlyn Gay and Sean McGarrahan, 2002.
3. *Stress Relief: The Ultimate Teen Guide,* by Mark Powell, 2002.
4. *Making Sexual Decisions: The Ultimate Teen Guide,* by L. Kris Gowen, Ph.D., 2003.
5. *Asthma: The Ultimate Teen Guide,* by Penny Hutchins Paquette, 2003.
6. *Cultural Diversity: Conflicts and Challenges: The Ultimate Teen Guide,* by Kathlyn Gay, 2003.
7. *Diabetes: The Ultimate Teen Guide,* by Katherine J. Moran, 2004.
8. *When Will I Stop Hurting? Teens, Loss, and Grief: The Ultimate Teen Guide,* by Edward Myers, 2004.
9. *Volunteering: The Ultimate Teen Guide,* by Kathlyn Gay, 2004.
10. *Organ Transplant: A Survival Guide for Recipients and Their Families: The Ultimate Teen Guide,* by Tina P. Schwartz, 2005.

Gender Identity

The Ultimate Teen Guide

CYNTHIA L. WINFIELD

It Happened to Me, No. 16

The Scarecrow Press, Inc.
Lanham, Maryland • Toronto • Plymouth, UK
2007

SCARECROW PRESS, INC.

Published in the United States of America
by Scarecrow Press, Inc.
A wholly owned subsidary of
The Rowman & Littlefield Publishing Group, Inc.
4501 Forbes Boulevard, Suite 200, Lanham, Maryland 20706
www.scarecrowpress.com

Estover Road
Plymouth PL6 7PY
United Kingdom

British Library Cataloguing in Publication Information Available

Library of Congress Cataloging-in-Publication Data

Winfield, Cynthia L., 1960–
  Gender identity : the ultimate teen guide / Cynthia L. Winfield.
     p. cm. — (It happened to me ; no. 16)
  Includes bibliographical references and index.
  ISBN-13: 978-0-8108-4907-5 (hardcover : alk. paper)
  ISBN-10: 0-8108-4907-0 (hardcover : alk. paper)
 1. Hermaphroditism—Social aspects. 2. Gender identity—United States. 3. Hermaphroditism—
Psychological aspects. 4. Gender identity—Social aspects. 5. Sexual orientation. I. Title.
RC883.W56 2007
616.6'9400835—dc22

                                                         2006021112

∞™ The paper used in this publication meets the minimum requirements of
American National Standard for Information Sciences—Permanence of Paper
for Printed Library Materials, ANSI/NISO Z39.48-1992.
Manufactured in the United States of America.

For all young people searching to find themselves,
their families, friends, and allies,
and the adults who work with and love them.
Also, for my beloved mother and father,
Evelyn Spencer Lees and Wayne Lowry Lees,
who have always loved me unconditionally,
and for my spouse, who has made my life whole.

Contents

HELPING PEOPLE UNDER-
STAND GENDER ISSUES
HELPS YOU, TOO

Acknowledgments

HELPING PEOPLE UNDER-
STAND GENDER ISSUES
HELPS YOU, TOO

NSSEXUAL
NSGENDER
HA

Although many resources were used to compile this book, in addition to the notes and resources some people deserve recognition.

Many thanks to Mickey Pearlman for giving my name to Arlene Hirschfelder, the "It Happened to Me" series editor. As well, heartfelt thanks to Arlene for recruiting me to write for this series, for her vision in recognizing this topic as pertinent, for seeing me through the many questions I had and the extensions I requested for the writing process, and for giving the manuscript such precise and deliberate attention. Sincere thanks to Phyllis Winfield, whose offhand suggestion one morning—"Why don't you do a book about gender?"— eclipsed my initial thoughts in the blink of an eye, and whose honest evaluation of the opening chapters served to shape the final piece. Genuine thanks to Denise LeClair, executive director of the International Foundation for Gender Education (IFGE), who made me feel welcome and who spent a couple of afternoons talking with me as I felt my way into this project. Respectful thanks to Mary Ann Horton, Ph.D., of Red Ace Consulting Services for designing the transition timelines and the ice cream cone chart, and for obtaining the transgender logo for me in a usable file format. Grateful thanks to Carol Feeney, middle school science teacher, for verifying science facts and for reviewing my words for accuracy, and to Patricia Lane, hawk-eyed friend, for her close reading of a late draft. Thanks to Julien Lamhene and Alice Winfrey Rutherford, young artists who worked with me for a time. Most sincere thanks to artist

Acknowledgments

Erin Lindsey, creator of the transgender comic strip *Venus Envy*, who worked this project into her busy schedule and created the characters Grant, Garret, Mikeala, and Tera specifically for *Gender Identity: The Ultimate Teen Guide*. And, many thanks to Linda Benson, book review editor at Voice of Youth Advocates, who thoughtfully shuttled books with lesbian/gay/bisexual/transgender (LGBT) themes my way for review.

A multitude of thanks to the young people—adults all, but young to me—who answered my call for submissions and opened their lives on paper for us to read. I would like to have included all of the submissions I received, but ultimately had to select those pieces most appropriate for this project. My earnest thanks to all of the young people who provided information and who spoke with me at length about their own gender identities.

As well, I wish to thank Grace Sterling Stowell, executive director of the Boston Alliance of Gay and Lesbian Youth (BAGLY), and Esther Morris Leidolf, founder and president of the Mayer Rotikansky Kuster Hauser Syndrome Organization (MRKH.org), for their informative presentations at the 2003 annual conference of the Gay, Lesbian, and Straight Educators Network, Boston Chapter (GLSEN Boston). Their talks about transgender and intersex issues, respectively, were readily accessible to the layperson, and their openness to continued dialogue was most helpful.

This project would not have been realized without the contributions made by all of you. Nor could it have gotten off the ground without all the authors and works cited within these pages or the myriad of Internet resources—such as the trans-youth web ring—available for teens and adults. Your pioneering works and sensitive, brave words are serving to make this world a better, more compassionate place—one in which I am proud to live. Thank you all so much.

Introduction

HELPING PEOPLE UNDER-
STAND GENDER ISSUES
HELPS YOU, TOO

Americans have long been fascinated by gender roles and those that extend beyond their expected boundaries, as evidenced by the number of cross-dressers and female impersonators in the early vaudeville, burlesque, and minstrel shows. The huge success of Finoccio's, a contemporary San Francisco club where men perform in drag, and similar clubs— like the one depicted in the 1996 movie *The Birdcage*, starring Nathan Lane and Robin Williams—speaks to our continued fascination with gender and our willingness to pay to view the successful undermining of our expectations. The contradiction of men appearing as women is compounded by the ability of some men to look quite attractive in a dress. But garnering an audience for theatrical productions is a far cry from achieving acceptance in daily life. Although our twenty-first-century society might like to imagine itself as having transcended many of the social limitations of our predecessors, gender identities, roles, and expectations still shape both our behaviors and people's perceptions of us.

From infancy, we are trained into one of two gender roles. Beginning with gender-colored Pampers and pastel pink or blue sleepers, we are socialized to fit either the "girl" role or the "boy" role. (While gender-neutral clothing items are available for infants and toddlers, they are far outnumbered by gender-specific items on the racks.) As we grow, we advance beyond simple color codes to basic social behavior patterns. Boys play war games and girls play house. Boys live rough-and-tumble existences; girls act with more sedate, demure manners.

Fifty years ago, in the mid-twentieth century, when societal roles were extremely rigid, boys played cops and robbers or engineered with train sets or building blocks, while girls played house or hopscotch or jumped rope. *Tomboys* were girls who avoided behaving like little ladies—perhaps preferring tree climbing to crocheting, and *sissies* were boys who behaved more like girls—perhaps playing with dolls instead of trucks; neither tomboys nor sissies were considered normal. Each had their place, but hopefully their place was not in *our own* family or neighborhood. While contemporary society allows boys and girls to play more equal roles, eyebrows are still raised when a boy from a working-class family studies ballet, or when a girl from an upper-class family desires to work as a truck driver, hauling loads long distances and often being away from home at night.

Indeed, usually the first question asked in the delivery room is about gender: "Is it a boy or a girl?" This seemingly innocuous question can be fraught with complications. More frequently than one might imagine, a baby is born with ambiguous genitalia, meaning the baby has *both* male and female sex characteristics. These children, who do not fit into society's boy–girl dichotomy, are properly called *intersex persons*, although many people erroneously refer to them as *hermaphrodites* (from the Latin *hermaphroditus* or Greek *hermaphroditos*, derived from *Hermaphroditos*).[1] Intersex births are nothing new. Historical writings and artifacts depict intersex individuals as early as the eleventh century B.C.E.[2] In Deuteronomy, a book from the Old Testament portion of the Bible, directives are given prohibiting cross-dressing and sex change. Such rules must have been written for a reason; they would not likely have appeared out of thin air. Indeed, one source conservatively estimates that as many as three to five children are born annually in each major American city with genitalia so ambiguous as to require genital surgery.[3]

Until quite recently, common practice has been for physicians to perform genital surgery once these infants are old enough to undergo such a major procedure, assigning the child what the doctor believes is his or her proper sex. What new parent is prepared to hear that her or his baby's sex is unclear?

At birth (or very close to it), children are assigned a gender. For the majority, the gender assigned fits the inner self and the body's physical appearance; for the intersex infant whose anatomy is confusing, the physician can offer genital surgery to eliminate ambiguity. The result of such surgery is removal of doubt; the postoperative child is anatomically male or female.

Viewing the arrival of an infant for whom the sex assignment is unclear as a medical emergency requiring treatment through genital surgery is a distinctly modern outlook. Medical experts who choose to perform genital surgery may believe they are acting in the child's best interest. But are they? Who is served when one human chooses a gender for another human, even when that choice is based upon observable primary and secondary sex characteristics? As well-meaning as the medical professionals may be, genital surgeries often rob the child of sensation in the area, require additional surgeries in the future, deliver the message to the child that he or she is somehow defective, and may produce a child whose gender, or biological sex, does not correspond to his or her internal gender identity. Do not all children deserve to be accepted and loved as they are?

Feelings of being different can be extremely isolating. Intersex children born with the expected anatomy, may not realize their intersexuality until later in life—often around puberty. Or, a person's internal sense of gender may not always agree with that designated by her or his external sexual equipment. In other words, sometimes a boy may feel that he is trapped inside the wrong body and that he is really a girl, or vice versa.

For many readers, language may add confusion to the discussion of trans issues. Sometimes "trans" appears as a prefix within a word; sometimes it stands alone, serving as an adjective. In other texts, readers may find some of the words written using hyphens. Below are some of the spellings used in this book, along with similarly configured words, to help readers understand my choices:

- heterosexual, bisexual, transsexual
- transgender

- gay person, straight person, trans person
- Native culture, Jewish culture, trans culture
- black community, trans community

Readers who find it helpful to mentally insert the pairing "transsexual/transgender" when encountering *trans* as a single whole word are encouraged to do so; I chose to use "trans" to make reading easier. Also, I use *transgender* in this text, although the words *transgender* and *transgendered* appear to be used almost interchangeably throughout the literature. When quoting other authors, I have let their spellings stand.

This book is about gender identity—the sense a person has of whether he or she is a boy or a girl—and what happens when this sense of self conflicts with the person's anatomical sex. After beginning with the classic case of "the boy who was raised as a girl," the book examines how hormones affect a developing fetus and how male and female brains may differ, considers the wealth of language that has grown up around these issues, investigates the presence and prevalence of intersex persons, briefly travels the road of transgender history—including current laws and protections—and concludes with ways anyone might help make the world a more understanding and accepting place for all of us, including those whose gender identity differs from the norm. Although issues faced by the trans community often overlap with those of the gay/lesbian/bisexual (GLB) community, and while the two communities are frequently lumped together as one—the gay/lesbian/bisexual/transgender (GLBT) community—this book is not about sexual identity. Additionally, although the intersex community is often included in the same mix— gay/lesbian/bisexual/transgender/intersex (GLBTI)—it has a different viewpoint and goals. That sexual minorities are lumped together provides convenient political alliances, but they represent at least three distinct communities, each with issues unique to it. For those interested in learning more about gender identity, a resource listing is provided following the text.

I hope readers will find the information on gender as fascinating as I have. You may never look at gender roles quite the same when you're through reading this book.

Enjoy your reading!

NOTES

1. In Greek mythology, Hermaphroditus, who rejected a nymph's love, was turned into a half-man/half-woman after the nymph asked the gods to unite them. The name is derived from the two gods, Hermes and Aphrodite, who were considered to be his parents.

2. B.C.E. stands for "before the common era" and is used as an alternative to B.C. ("before Christ"). Similarly, A.D., from the Latin *Anno Domini* ("in the year of the Lord"), is often replaced by C.E. or "common era."

3. John Colapinto, *As Nature Made Him: The Boy Who Was Raised as a Girl* (New York: HarperCollins, 2000), 75–76.

1

Dr. Money's Conclusive Case

HELPING PEOPLE UNDER-
STAND GENDER ISSUES
HELPS YOU, TOO

SPECIAL DELIVERY: TWIN BOYS

The classic case of "the boy who was raised as a girl" deserves consideration because it directly influenced current medical policy and practice. The story begins with David Reimer, who did not always use that name. He was born a normal, healthy boy but—as the result of a tragic childhood accident—was raised as a girl for most of his first fourteen years of life.[1] At birth he was named Bruce, and he spent much of his childhood with the name Brenda. During this time, he felt he was a boy, but for reasons that he could not understand and were beyond his control, the adults around him treated him as though he were a girl—causing him much confusion and psychological discomfort. His story begins in the mid-1960s.

On August 22, 1965, identical twin boys, the first named Bruce and the second, born twelve minutes later, named Brian, were born four weeks prematurely at Saint Boniface Hospital in Winnipeg, Canada. Their proud parents were Ron and Janet Reimer, a young couple who had completed their education through grades seven and nine, respectively, and who fell in love as teens. They married when Janet became pregnant just after her eighteenth birthday, and shortly before Ron's twentieth. Both of them, raised in strict Mennonite homes (a form of Christianity), had become estranged from their own parents as they matured into twentieth-century youth culture. Thus, Bruce and Brian's young parents lacked guidance from more mature adults as they undertook the task of raising their two boys.

Thankfully, although the boys arrived four weeks prematurely, they were born healthy and normal.

ROUTINE ILLNESS: HARBINGER OF TRAGEDY

When the boys were seven months old, they both developed a condition called *phimosis*, which caused the foreskins on their penises to close, making urination difficult and painful. The parents were told that having routine circumcisions could help relieve their sons of the condition. Circumcision is a surgical procedure where the foreskin is removed from the penis, depriving the organ of its protective shroud, and—some believe—providing a cleaner environment less prone to infection. The procedure is routinely performed on male Jewish

CIRCUMCISION: WHO DECIDES?

Although some parents have their baby boys circumcised for religious reasons, others have the procedure performed for reasons of hygiene or health, or so the son will resemble his father. Medical views on circumcision have varied over the years. The American Academy of Pediatrics (AAP) has published several policy statements on the topic during the last four decades. In the 1971 AAP manual, *Standards and Recommendations of Hospital Care of Newborn Infants*, and in its 1975 and 1983 revisions, the Academy found no absolute medical reason for having the procedure performed. But newer research on urinary tract infections and sexually transmitted diseases, including AIDS, led the Academy to conclude, in a 1989 policy statement, that circumcision had potential medical benefits and advantages, as well as risks and disadvantages. Since then, medical societies in various parts of the developed world have stated that routine infant male circumcision is not recommended.[2]

In 1999, statistics gathered in the United States showed that about two-thirds of both white and black male infants were circumcised as infants, but that the number of circumcisions varied widely by geographic region. Babies in the Midwest were far more likely to have the procedure performed than were babies in the South or West.[3]

infants in a ritual *bris* ceremony, on Muslims as a form of spiritual purification, and on other infants at their parents' request. The couple decided to have Bruce and Brian circumcised.

At eight months, the Reimer boys were readmitted to Saint Boniface Hospital for routine circumcisions. Experienced pediatricians at this large teaching hospital successfully performed about a thousand of these procedures each year. But on the morning the Reimer boys were scheduled for surgery, Dr. Jean-Marie Huot, a general practitioner, was the covering physician. When he performed the procedure on the first twin, Bruce, Dr. Huot employed an unusual method that involved an electrocautery machine—with disastrous results. The surgery left baby Bruce's penis damaged beyond repair. The younger twin's procedure was canceled, and Brian fully recovered from phimosis within weeks. Unfortunately, Bruce's circumcision was so "botched" that within a few days, "baby Bruce's penis dried and broke away in pieces. [Soon] all vestiges of the organ were gone completely."[4] Bruce's bladder drained through a tube exiting his body below the belly button. Ron and Janet were told that phallic reconstruction (the rebuilding of Bruce's penis) would result in a penis that not only looked strange but also lacked the capacity either to feel or to become erect. Baby Bruce remained in the hospital for weeks, and when his devastated parents finally brought him home, they had not made a decision about additional surgery.

A POSSIBLE SOLUTION

Nearly a year later, the parents still had not chosen to have phallic reconstructive surgery for Bruce. Then one day while watching a television talk show, they listened to a medical expert discuss his work with intersex children and gender identity. Dr. John Money, a medical psychologist with the Johns Hopkins Psychohormonal Research Unit in Baltimore, Maryland, spoke about his research team's success performing male-to-female sexual reassignments. He claimed to be able not only to change a person's genitals from male to female but also to help the patient feel comfortable with her new sex assignment. He was certain that boys having the surgery within the first two-and-a-half years of life could successfully be raised as girls. Dr. Money reported successful experiences doing this for a number of infants who had been born with at least partially formed genitals of both sexes. He said that his work allowed these intersex children to live happy, normal lives.

Viewing the show, Ron and Janet were impressed. Believing that Dr. Money could be the savior their family needed, they hung onto his every word.

DISCOVER FOR YOURSELF

You can find David Reimer's biography in your local library or order it through a bookstore. It is entitled *As Nature Made Him: The Boy Who Was Raised as a Girl* by John Colapinto (New York: HarperCollins, 2000).

Troubled by their one-and-a-half-year-old's missing penis, the parents were enthralled by Dr. Money's televised presentation, as well as his personality, energy, and drive. "The world's undisputed authority on the psychological ramifications of ambiguous genitalia"[5] spoke emphatically about his belief that a child could be raised comfortably in either gender, so long as the gender identity was established before the child reached two and a half years of age. For intersex infants, Dr. Money had been routinely recommending transsexual surgeries, which were performed by his surgical team; although the work of this serious and groundbreaking researcher was lauded at the time, eventually some of Dr. Money's theories would prove to be tragically wrong. Of course, ambiguous genitalia were not Bruce's problem; he had very clearly been born a healthy, normal boy. Even so, the Reimers believed that Dr. Money's research might prove to be the answer to the family's prayers. They contacted the Johns Hopkins clinic promptly.

For the research team at Johns Hopkins, of which Dr. Money was a member, the opportunity to reassign the sex of a baby born as a normal boy, who had an identical twin not in

STARRING: HOLLYWOOD
Watch cinema marquees for the arrival of David Reimer's story. Peter Jackson (the New Zealand writer and director of the "Lord of the Rings" movie trilogy) purchased the movie rights to Colapinto's book *As Nature Made Him*, and in 2004 DreamWorks was said to be developing a screenplay of the story.[6]

need of surgery, was enormously exciting. Such an "unplanned opportunity" that could confirm their conclusions later came to be "highlighted as [Money's] most impressive accomplishment in sex and gender research."[7] The charismatic doctor told the Reimers about the procedure, which they understood to have been performed before—although Bruce would in fact be the first clearly male child to be made female; the Johns Hopkins team had previously performed sex reassignment surgeries only on intersex children.[8] The parents did not understand that, for a child born normally, the surgery was experimental. They also did not know about Dr. Milton Diamond, a graduate student in Kansas whose work published in 1965 questioned Money's theories. Nor were they aware that Diamond believed that gender identity is formed in the womb. Diamond's assertion about the strength of biological or hereditary causes (nature) contrasted with Money's theory that gender identity is formed through children's interactions with their environment (nurture). The Reimers remained unaware of the "nature" side of the argument.

TERMINOLOGY

Intersex is a condition where a baby is born with male and female sex characteristics. The word *hermaphrodite* was used for many years to describe intersex persons, often understood by the layperson as describing one born with complete sex organs that are both male and female, but this connotation is erroneous. Indeed the biology of human development should make this impossible (see chapter 4). While the word *hermaphrodite* can still be heard, avoid incorporating it into your working vocabulary. Currently this word is viewed as a pejorative, or derogatory, term and *intersex* is the preferred word to use.

BRUCE BECOMES BRENDA

Upon returning home after their first meeting with Dr. Money, Ron and Janet agreed to change Bruce's gender from male to female. Bruce became Brenda within the critical two-and-a-half-year window identified by Money's research team. Once the parents were convinced that a surgical sex change was their son's only choice, the toddler underwent physical castration at the Johns Hopkins Hospital and was no longer a biological male. With longer hair, frilly dresses, dolls, and positive reinforcement for female behaviors, Brenda should have made the transition to girlhood smoothly, according to Money's theory. However, despite Ron and Janet's efforts, little Brenda continued to gravitate toward "boy toys" and behaviors. Even so, Janet Reimer aided the renowned doctor by reporting every instance of feminine behavior by her older son. Subsequently, when both twins visited Johns Hopkins annually for psychological testing and interviews, Bruce's masculine tendencies escaped Money's notice.

When Brenda entered school, her teachers noticed that something was amiss. Sex differences often become more obvious as children enter school and choose to group themselves according to gender-specific interests. These differences become especially obvious on the playground. Brenda's kindergarten and first-grade teachers were confused because Brenda was distinctly boyish. While her play appeared to be gender-specific, she did not choose "girl activities." She

EXPLORE FURTHER

The PBS television series *NOVA* aired an episode in 2001 titled "Sex: Unknown," which documents David Reimer's case in light of continuing medical research and theory. Prominent sex researchers, including Dr. Milton Diamond, explain their theories. The Reimers present their personal experiences. No one from the Johns Hopkins Hospital was available to comment in the film.

even urinated standing up, which was a messy business because she could not aim like a boy. Her parents could no longer keep her secret, and school personnel became understanding once the girl's surgical history was explained to them. Brenda, though, remained confused. Not having the surgeries explained to her, she continued to believe she was Brian's brother even though adults always treated her as a girl.

Her doctor saw no reason for Brenda to be confused. When she was six years old, he publicized her case. Based upon the children's annual sojourns to Johns Hopkins and periodic reports from her parents, Dr. Money published his landmark text *Man & Woman, Boy & Girl* in 1972, wherein he reported Brenda's transformation to be a total success.[9] This claim was repeated when Money presented his findings at an American Association for the Advancement of Science (AAAS) meeting. The twins' study provided irrefutable evidence; Brenda had been born male, with no ambiguity, and her transition to girlhood was said to be entirely successful. Money's assertion that gender identity is solely the result of environment was made so convincingly that sexual reassignment surgery became a standardized practice in the United States and abroad.

But Brenda continued to have a difficult childhood. By the time she was eight years old, Brenda envisioned herself as a boy. That year, Money wanted to complete her surgical transformation by constructing a vagina for her, but the child adamantly refused further surgery at Johns Hopkins. She feared that the surgery would remove completely the existence of the boy she knew herself to be. While the psychological interviews with Dr. Money continued for a few more years, and even after other doctors contacted him with their findings about Brenda's identification as a boy, no refutation of his initial claim was ever published. When he looked at Brenda, Dr. Money saw a girl.

In school, Brenda found it increasingly difficult to fit in, and her family members suffered as well. Her masculine behaviors made her an oddity. Unable to make friends, Brenda often experienced ridicule by her peers. The Reimer family went so far as to move to British Columbia seeking a geographical cure, but the relocation found the parents estranged from each other. Ron was drinking more, and Janet was seriously depressed. In time, the Reimers returned east to Winnipeg. Although those around Brenda could see something was seriously wrong, no adult chose to question the renowned Dr. Money. According to John Colapinto's *As Nature Made Him: The Boy Who Was Raised as a Girl*, the Johns Hopkins doctor's conclusions were readily accepted. He continued reporting success with Brenda's case. One psychotherapist who did question Money's "successful" treatment was summarily dismissed from the case. Later, when other clinicians wrote to Money to report how Brenda's transformation was not working, he glossed over their concerns.

ADOLESCENCE INCREASES GENDER CONFUSION

Brenda reached puberty; her shoulders widened and her voice began to change. Brenda's new psychotherapist urged the Reimers to tell their "daughter" the truth. The parents addressed the matter, without elaboration. Ron spoke of an accident, of a doctor's mistake "down there," and the family dropped the matter without making clear to Brenda that she had been born male. A local physician agreed to start Brenda on her scheduled estrogen therapy, to provide the female hormone her body required in order to develop into womanhood. With the estrogen, Brenda's hips and waist became more rounded and she grew breasts. Uncomfortable with these changes, Brenda indulged in eating binges, using fat to cloak her burgeoning womanhood. Over the fat, she dressed like a boy.

In middle school, Brenda found she could fit in with other misfit students. She developed a fast friendship with a girl named Heather. This new friend noticed differences between Brenda and herself. While Heather, a masculine female, wanted to be *like* boys, Brenda wanted to *be* a boy. Heather did not fight physically with boys; Brenda both wanted to and did fight boys. Then the Reimers took Brenda for one final visit to Johns Hopkins, despite her tantrums that took place each visit. There Brenda received a pep talk from a male-to-female transsexual. This spooked the young teen, who perceived the transsexual as a man wearing makeup and women's clothing, speaking in a higher-than-male voice. Brenda ran from that interview, and later told her mother that she would kill herself before returning to Johns Hopkins and Dr. Money.

THE TRUTH COMES OUT

When Brenda reached age fourteen, her doctors in Winnipeg decided the time had arrived when she must be told about her surgical history. Based on the information she had previously been given, Brenda had been operating under the assumption that her mother had beaten her "down there" when she was very young. While Janet explained to Brian, Ron told Brenda the truth in its entirety. He explained that "she" had been born as a healthy, normal boy, the elder twin, but in a circumcision gone awry, the penis had been burned so badly that it broke off within days. He related how he and Janet had been devastated by the accident, especially when they were told Bruce could never lead the life of a normal male. Ron told Brenda how Dr.

Money's work had offered the parents a way to give their baby a normal life.

Brenda was relieved to learn the basis of the conflicting feelings with which she had been struggling all of her life. Understandably, she was furious with Dr. Huot, the general practitioner who had performed her circumcision. But she also knew what she wanted: She would lead life as a man.

DAVID

The transition was not easy. Brenda selected the name David. A strong biblical name, David represented the triumph of good over evil—like David who slew the giant Goliath. David now had his male future ahead of him, a troubled past only recently behind him, and the realization that he could never have children. His estrogen therapy was replaced by testosterone injections. Then he had a double mastectomy—both of David's breasts were removed. The surgery was so traumatic and painful that he put off further surgeries.

While the teens were still living at home, both twins and their mother battled depression and suicidal feelings. When one girl in whom David confided made his secrets public, his response was to attempt suicide. When David's parents initially found him following that suicide attempt (the first of two), they debated between themselves whether to intervene. They felt their child had faced more than a lifetime's share of adversity already and wondered if it would be kinder to let him go. Very quickly, though, they elected to save their son's life. Later, David chose to undergo two phalloplasty surgeries to build a functional penis. Medical science had advanced considerably since his initial accident, and finally David approximated a "normal" male.

The twins grew up and moved on, out of their parents' home and into society. When Brian married and fathered two children, David became sure that marriage and fatherhood were the future he wanted as well. He decided that if he could find a single mother with whom he was compatible, he could have children in his life and be a father. He had many fears to conquer, but when Jane entered his life, his world was complete.

A single mother of three young children with a heart big enough to include David, she was indeed the answer to his prayers.

David Reimer eventually chose to make his story public in hopes of saving other children from a similar plight. Even though Dr. Money changed his opinion about the nature-versus-nurture argument and, until his death in 2006, stood firmly behind biology as being the stronger force, his groundbreaking work with intersex children and with the Reimer case—wherein he claimed success publicly for years—helped to make genital surgery a standard procedure in hospitals across the country and around the world. At the turn of the twenty-first century, the surgery was "performed in virtually every major country with the possible exception of China."[10]

For some reason, statistics on the number of genital surgeries done on infants have not been kept. One doctor estimates there may well be a thousand of them performed around the globe annually.[11] Statistics drawn from an article by Dr. Anne Fausto-Sterling, a Brown University professor, assert that one or two of every 1,000 babies will undergo surgery to "normalize" the appearance of their genitals,[12] while an article in *The Scientist* states that one in 2,000 babies are candidates for such surgery.[13]

As stories such as David's are told completely, and groups such as the Intersex Society of North America (ISNA) actively seek to educate the medical community, the standards are slowly changing (see appendix A).[14] Surgery for children with genital ambiguities is no longer automatic, and more parents are included in the decision making. Medical centers are beginning to address the complexity of these cases, and some

DISCOVER FOR YOURSELF

The Intersex Society of North America (ISNA), an organization that works to educate people about intersex issues, is an excellent resource for readers seeking technical information and more in-depth discussions of intersex issues. See their website at www.isna.org.

medical schools are teaching alternatives to early genital surgery.[15] Although the impact of Dr. Money's initial research findings has been far-reaching, as medical professionals become familiar with the unintended consequences of these early surgeries, and the public becomes aware of the prevalence of intersex conditions (see chapter 4), fewer children may undergo genital surgery before they are of age to take part in the decision.

David Reimer died May 4, 2004, at age thirty-eight. He committed suicide. His twin, Brian Reimer, had committed suicide two years earlier. David left behind a wife (from whom he was separated) and three children, as well as his parents. His obituary was widely published.

NOTES

1. This chapter draws extensively from John Colapinto's biography of David Reimer, *As Nature Made Him: The Boy Who Was Raised as a Girl* (New York: HarperCollins, 2000).

2. American Academy of Pediatrics, Task Force on Circumcision, "Circumcision Policy Statement," *Pediatrics* 103, no. 3 (March 1999): 686–93, also available at http://aappolicy.aappublications.org/cgi/content/full/pediatrics;103/3/686.

3. U.S. Department of Health and Human Services, Centers for Disease Control and Prevention, National Center for Health Statistics, "Trends in Circumcisions among Newborns," www.cdc.gov/nchs/products/pubs/pubd/hestats/circumcisions/circumcisions.htm.

4. Colapinto, *As Nature Made Him*, 15.

5. Colapinto, *As Nature Made Him*, 25.

6. Moonhawk River Stone, "OPPS . . . A Word from the Chair of the IFGE Board of Directors, Moonhawk River Stone," *Transgender Tapestry*, no. 107 (2004): 7.

7. Colapinto, *As Nature Made Him*, 78. This assessment came from a 1974 biographical profile of Dr. Money run in Baltimore's *News American* newspaper.

8. "Sex: Unknown," *NOVA*, PBS Television, 2001. Additional related resources are available at www.pbs.org/wgbh/nova/gender.

9. To protect the Reimer family's privacy, Money used the pseudonyms John and Joan in place of Bruce and Brenda.

10. Colapinto, *As Nature Made Him*, 75.

11. Colapinto, *As Nature Made Him*, 76.

12. Intersex Society of North America, "Frequency: How Common Are Intersex Conditions?" www.isna.org/faq/frequency.html.

13. Ricki Lewis, "Reevaluating Sex Reassignment," *Scientist* 14, no. 14 (10 July 2000): 6.

14. Although the ISNA is cited throughout this book, the statements made herein are those of the author and impart the author's interpretation of material; they do not represent ISNA's position on any of these issues, nor are they meant to do so.

15. Mireya Navarro, "When Gender Isn't a Given," *New York Times*, Sunday Styles section, 19 September 2004.

Trans History through the Ages and across Cultures

2

Transgenderism is not a new phenomenon, although the *concept* of transgender is relatively new. Indeed, transgender people have been with us for centuries, and perhaps for as long as any people have roamed the Earth. Biblical laws against transvestism appear in Deuteronomy: "A woman shall not wear anything that pertains to a man, nor shall a man put on a woman's garment; for whosoever does these things is an abomination to the Lord your God" (22:5). Deuteronomy 23:1 further states: "He whose testicles are crushed or whose male member is cut off shall not enter the assembly of the Lord." Although the date these laws were laid down is uncertain, they were written before the sixth century B.C.E. Clearly the taboos against crossing gender roles have been part of human society for thousands of years—and why include such rules unless someone crossed a boundary for acceptable gender role behavior during ancient times?

TRANSGENDER HISTORICAL FIGURES

In the fifteenth century B.C.E., Egypt was ruled for more than twenty years by King Hatchepsut, a woman who served her country in the role of its divine pharaoh. Alternately remembered in history as queen or king, Hatchepsut preferred to be viewed as male and successfully conducted business as pharaoh during Egypt's 18th dynasty. Dressing as a king, Hatchepsut's attire included the pharaoh's traditional fake beard. Although much of Hatchepsut's rule has been lost to history, and while she is often depicted as a traditional king, some remaining statuary shows her dressed as a male but having distinctly female breasts.[1]

In the fifteenth century C.E., during the Hundred Years' War in France, a seventeen-year-old female peasant donned the garb of military men, mounted a horse, and ultimately rode to sainthood in the eyes of her adoring public. Her stated goal was to lead an army of peasants and expel the occupying English troops. This woman, known to us as Joan of Arc, incited furor and fear among members of the ruling class; in time, she saw Prince Charles crowned as King of France. Shortly thereafter, she was captured by allies of the English feudal lords. But because her role as a successful female military leader of peasants actually threatened the French nobility whom she had helped gain power, the nobles declined to come to her aid. Denounced for her gender identity and expression—not just her cross-dressing, but her cross-gendered appearance in general— Joan spoke on her own behalf at the trial held by the Inquisition. At her hearings, Joan was accused of "following the custom of the Gentiles and the Heathen."[2] She refused to take an oath that she would stop acting and dressing as a man, and so Joan of Arc was burned at the stake in 1431; she was nineteen.

If the peasantry prized transgender expression, only to face brutal punishments as did Joan of Arc, the wealthy and powerful did not. As continues to be true today, wealth buys one a certain amount of social comfort and behavioral latitude denied to persons in poverty. A wealthy eccentric is just that—a wealthy eccentric—but an impoverished eccentric is often seen as deviant. The word *deviant* carries only negative connotations, while the word *eccentric* implies deviance but has connotations that include a measure of tolerance or acceptance and understanding for the individual who is different.

Throughout history, the unusual behavior of the wealthy and powerful has been tolerated. In the sixteenth century, King Henry III of France often cross-dressed. When the king was dressed as a woman, courtiers referred to him as "her majesty." In the seventeenth century, Queen Christina of Sweden relinquished her throne in order to dress as a man; she renamed herself Count Dohna. In the same century, the woman Nzinga ruled as King of Angola for nearly three decades. In the 1670s, the male-to-female transsexual Abbe Francois Timoleon de Choisy attended the pope's inaugural ball dressed as a woman; his memoirs provide the earliest first-person documentation of cross-dressing.

In the early nineteenth century, the renowned French author George Sand, a female who often wore men's clothes, was as famous for her affairs as for her writing. She scandalized her peers by being the first woman in modern European history to dress this way. Toward mid-century, in Wales, a group of male-to-female cross-dressers banded together in Robin Hood fashion, calling themselves "Rebecca and her daughters." Much like Robin Hood's merry men, the Rebeccas destroyed road toll barriers to benefit the poor. Later in the century, during the U.S. Civil War, female-to-male cross-dressing flourished, as women who wished to serve the cause disguised themselves as men to join the fight. Upon their deaths, about 400 soldiers, on both the Union and Confederate sides, were found to be women.[3]

Today, although the male/female gender role dichotomy continues to thrive in U.S. culture, other cultures—both on this continent and around the world—recognize, accept, and even celebrate transgender persons. *Eunuchs*, the name derived from the Greek *eunoukhos* or bedroom guard, were castrated males given important historical roles. Employed as harem attendants or charged with important affairs of state in Asian courts and under the Roman emperors, these emasculated males held favored positions in royal households. The *hijras* of India, whose history dates back 2,500 years, are known as a "third gender" caste today. While some hijras are born intersex, others choose to become hijra. Although mostly marginalized by society, hijras bless children and exercise symbolic powers in Indian culture.[4] In Europe, the *castrati* (from the Italian *castrare*, to castrate) were adult male singers who had been castrated in their youth to retain a childlike soprano or alto voice. The *mahu* of Hawaii were respected before Christianity came to the islands, and while they are far less visible today,

EXPLORE FURTHER: *TABOO*
The National Geographic Channel series *Taboo* examines cultural taboos around the globe. In the "Gender Benders" episode (aired in 2004), three sets of gender benders appear: female body builders in the United States, brides of India's Koovagam Festival, and Japanese female wrestlers.

they continue to have a role in Hawaiian culture. Author Andrew Matzner, in his book *'O Au No Keia: Voices from Hawaii's Mahu and Transgender Communities* (2001), shares the stories of contemporary mahu and their attempts to reflect the diversity of the community. In the Dominican Republic, the *guevedoche* are recognized as a third sex. Born with a rare form of pseudo-hermaphroditism, they are often assumed to be female at birth but develop male characteristics at puberty (much like the character of Cal Stephanides in Jeffrey Eugenides's 2002 novel *Middlesex*). In fact, the name *guevedoche* translates to "balls at twelve."[5]

ANNUAL FESTIVAL IN KOOVAGAM, INDIA

Each April, as part of an annual ritual in the town of Koovagam, India, thousands of men gather to honor the warrior-god Aravan, whose life was sacrificed in order to win a war.[6] Dressed as brides, they ceremonially wed their god-husband and remain his new bride for the night. Although hijras live at the margins of Indian society, in which conversation about cross-dressing is taboo and homosexuality can result in imprisonment, this annual ceremony celebrates the brief marriage of the eunuch Aravan to the god Krishna. Krishna is said to have temporarily transformed into a woman for the marriage, and then had Aravan beheaded the next day. Men of all sexual orientations partake in this ritual. Homosexuals, bisexuals, transvestites, hijras, and even heterosexual men who have wives and children wear dresses, makeup, and jewelry for the celebration.

While some people see this behavior as bizarre and may offer ridicule or catcalls, hordes of male "sexual tourists" also flock to the town for the Koovagam Festival. There, they are ceremonially wed to one of the temporary brides, and although the "marriage" lasts only for the night, and one or both parties entering into this ceremonial union may already be married, it is understood that their marriage will be consummated that night. In the morning, the brides have their jewelry and garlands of flowers cut off and become widows who return to their usual lives. For those who live on the fringes of society throughout the year, this annual ritual provides affirmation and a place where they can belong.

NATIVE AMERICAN TWO-SPIRIT PEOPLE

On this continent, Native American cultures recognize that gender is not simply an either/or male/female occurrence. Just as a diversity of Native American cultures exists, so too the Native views of gender encompass diversity—and they do seem to agree that transgender, or "other than either male or female," is an option. In Native culture, the *berdache* or two-spirit individual is accepted as a third sex. In fact, transgender Natives were often respected or revered and held positions of power in the tribe. The tribal *shamans*, or healers, were frequently transgender individuals. Examples of Native views of gender roles can be found throughout all tribes, and given the vast number of tribal languages, many words exist to describe transgender Native people.

Among the Navajo people, gender was not assigned when a child of indeterminate gender was born. Rather, they allowed the child a voice in the determination of its own gender in an unusual ritual. In her book *Gender Outlaw*, Kate Bornstein relates that "when the gender of a child was in question . . . , they reached a decision by putting a child inside a *tipi* with [a] loom and a bow and arrow—female and male implements respectively. They set fire to the *tipi*, and whatever the child grabbed as he/she ran out determined the child's gender."[7] Furthermore, in Navajo culture the *nadle* is a kind of transgender male-to-female individual whose social role is antifeminist. Bornstein notes that the nadle "was often called upon to suppress women's revolutions."[8] This makes sense when one considers that throughout history those in power have coerced the oppressed to join forces with them and further oppress their own.

When the Europeans came to colonize the Americas, they used *berdache* as a derogatory word to describe any Native person who did not fit their narrow gender role expectations. As the colonizers explored the Americas, reports of transgender Native peoples were common, and often disparaging. In time, the European colonizers sought to impose their own standards of behavior upon Native peoples. As we know today, their efforts at colonization amounted to genocide and extreme cultural suppression.

The imposition of European or Christian standards did not end when the United States achieved independence from British rule. In the 1850s, white Western travelers to Montana and Wyoming were shocked to encounter Barcheeampe, the Crow nation "woman chief" who was famous both for prowess in war and for polygamy. In 1886, We'wha, a six-foot-tall two-spirit Zuni artisan (see figure 2.1), is reported to have visited President Grover Cleveland in Washington, D.C., without being recognized by the president as having been born male.[9] In the late nineteenth century, the U.S. government subjected the Crow nation's *badé* (or *boté*) to demeaning treatment and punishment in its attempts to change their behavior.[10] Although today the term *berdache* is not generally derogatory, Native peoples may prefer that the gentler, more compassionate term "two-spirit" be used to describe persons having diverse gender expressions.[11]

Figure 2.1.   We'wha, a Native American (Zuni), weaves a belt on a backstrap loom, Zuni Pueblo, New Mexico. We'wha is a *berdache*, a man who prefers women's work and adopts female dress; he is dressed as a woman and wears a woven manta, moccasins, and squash blossom necklace. *(Denver Public Library, Western History Collection; History of the American West, 1860–1920; Reproduction Number X-30150)*

EXPLORE FURTHER: GENDER IN NATIVE AMERICAN CULTURES

Learn more about Native American *berdache* people through books such as these:

- *The Spirit and the Flesh* by Walter Williams (Boston: Beacon Press, 1986) chronicles nearly as many types of berdache people as there were different tribes! An important milestone in trans cultural history, this book includes the voices of Native two-spirit people.
- *Changing Ones: Third and Fourth Genders in Native North America* by Will Roscoe (New York: St. Martin's Press, 1998) provides a comprehensive exploration of the tribal roles of berdache native North Americans.
- An earlier work by Roscoe, *The Zuni Man-Woman* (Albuquerque: University of New Mexico Press, 1991) reveals the story of We'wha (see figure 2.1) and examines berdache roles among the Pueblo Indians.

Although Native Americans allow for gender diversity, throughout the history of the United States, diversity of either sexual preference or gender within the settlers' population has always been viewed as suspect. (Figure 2.2 documents one of the early punishments for homosexuality as practiced in Colorado.) However, a tradition of transgender expression does

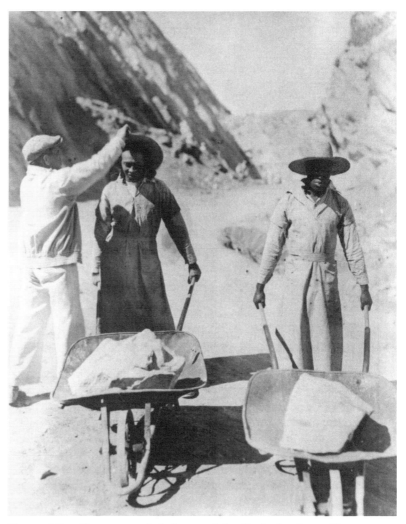

Figure 2.2. **Homosexuals being punished by being forced to wear dresses and straw hats while wheeling heavy rocks at the State Penitentiary in Canon City, Colorado. A man lifts the hat of one of the prisoners. The shadowed faces of the prisoners lend an air of anonymity, and a sense that anyone could be made to stand in their shoes.** *(Denver Public Library, Western History Collection; History of the American West, 1860–1920; Reproduction Number X-77770)*

appear as part of certain U.S. holiday celebrations such as Mardi Gras, mummers' parades, and Halloween.

GENDER IN THE TWENTIETH CENTURY

The Institute for Sexual Science in Germany was founded in 1919 by sexologist and homosexual reformer Magnus Hirschfeld (1868–1935), who described homosexuals as "the third sex." Hirschfeld, a known cross-dresser, also coined the term *transvestite*. By the end of his life, the climate toward gender-variant individuals had become distinctly frostier.

> In 1936, Heinrich Himmler, Reichsführer SS and head of the Gestapo, told the Germans: "Just as we today have gone back to the ancient Germanic view on the question of marriage mixing different races, so too in our judgment of homosexuality—a symptom of degeneracy which could destroy our race—we must return to the guiding Nordic principle: extermination of degenerates." . . . Although the Nazi Party had always been officially anti-gay, in its early years many [opposing groups] lampooned them as homosexual. Hitler's 15-year friendship with the chief of staff of the SA (*Sturmabteilung*—storm troopers or "Brown Shirts"), Ernst Röhm—who was publicly known to be gay after he appeared in court on homosexuality charges in 1925—lent credence to this propaganda.[12]

Although homosexuals were targeted by the Nazis during World War II and vilified and ostracized elsewhere in the world, transsexuals were practically invisible to society—of necessity. Then, in 1952, an ex-GI from the Bronx underwent transsexual surgery in Sweden and became the center of a media circus for some time. Christine Jorgensen's sex change operation made headlines around the world. News of her sex change titillated the public, but her story signaled to many transgender people, who may have felt uncomfortably different and isolated, that they were not alone. In her introduction to Cleis Press's 2001 reissue of Jorgensen's autobiography, Susan Stryker writes:

> Fate placed Christine Jorgensen in the limelight, but her own talent and charisma kept her there. She threw herself heart and

soul into playing the part of the world's first famous transsexual: educating and entertaining, being gracious and glamourous, striving for the respect that every individual should be given as a birthright.[13]

Jorgensen's life provided hope and inspiration for other transgender and transsexual people.

Some transgender people manage to avoid detection. When Billy Tipton, a notable jazz musician and band leader of the 1940s and 1950s, died in 1989, his female body surprised the medical technicians who had arrived on the scene. Tipton had lived for more than half a century as a man, was married a number of times, and raised children—although he neither fathered nor bore the children—all successfully. For readers who imagine his wives *must* have known, consider how well a person's modesty was respected at the time, and how a clever man—who was perhaps shy and liked the lights turned down—could pull off such a stunt. If you're still skeptical, or simply curious, the biography of Tipton's life, *Suits Me* (1998), would be a good place to start; it includes quotes from people who knew Billy well.

TRANSGENDER POLITICS

History was made in July 2004 at the Democratic National Convention (DNC) in Boston when, for the first time, a contingent of openly transgender delegates attended. Although one delegate had identified as such in the past, 2004 brought a contingent of five. They wore special DNC buttons incorporating a U.S. flag, a Revolutionary War silhouette, and a prominently displayed transgender logo.

Some transgender people pass successfully for a time, only to be outed in their lifetimes. One of the beautiful women from the James Bond movies, Carolyn "Tula" Cossey, worked as an actress and model until she was outed by the British press late in the 1980s. Watch *For Your Eyes Only*; can you pick out which Bond Girl she is?

Overall, the second half of the twentieth century brought a greater openness to and visibility of gender bending. Transvestism hit prime time, and in such a way that many viewers supported cross-dressing by TV characters. The character Corporal Klinger on *M*A*S*H* (1972–83) dressed in women's clothes hoping for a "Section 8" discharge from the military. Viewers knew his behavior only served to prove his sanity to the psychiatrist who periodically visited the 4077th Mobile Army Surgical Hospital near the Korean War front. In the early 1980s, *Bosom Buddies*, a popular television sitcom, featured two heterosexual, masculine young men who cross-dressed in order to secure housing. By the time the sitcom *Ally McBeal* hit the airwaves in 1997, the show starring a single lawyer with eccentric colleagues featured transgender characters who were "portrayed with understanding, pathos, and acceptance."[14]

By the 1990s, a full-scale gender revolution was under way. This is not to say that gender bending and gender blending are wholly accepted in society. But if you think for a minute, you can probably name a handful of transgender people who are thriving in public view. With the publication of John Berendt's history of Savannah, Georgia, *Midnight in the Garden of Good and Evil* (1994), Lady Chablis achieved national acclaim and a good measure of respect. Dr. Renée Richards, a world-class tennis player who competed as a woman following her transition, now has a successful career as an ophthalmic surgeon. Jenny Boylan, an English professor from Colby College, wrote of her transition in *She's Not There: A Life in Two Genders*. Acclaimed musical performer RuPaul stuns audiences with her presentation as a hot, sexy woman. Similarly, Kate Bornstein, transsexual lesbian performance artist, enjoys a successful career in the public eye. Even the former arranger and keyboard player for the 1970s band Jethro Tull, David Palmer, announced his gender switch after the death of his wife; in his mid-sixties, he became "Dee."[15]

On the islands of Hawaii there exists a cultural melting pot with Hawaiian, Filipino, Japanese, Chinese, Laotian, Portuguese, and Polynesian cultures as the basis, though the resulting mix has been heavily influenced by Western and Christian ways. The stories in Andrew Matzner's book (see sidebar) reflect how these later influences impacted the visibility of Hawaii's mahu population. The narratives relate not only each person's current reality but also much cultural history about the Hawaiian Islands.

At one time, Hawaiians viewed gender along a continuum that was inclusive of differences. They believed everyone is born androgynous and that as we mature either the male or female side becomes stronger, more prominent— except in mahu, who develop their male and female strengths equally. Thus, the mahu were seen as strong people; they could do all the things that both men and women do and were not restricted by identifying with just one gender. As for sexuality, "bisexualism was the norm. Hawaiians loved whomever loved them. . . . If they felt *aloha* for somebody then they loved them."[16] Futher, mahu were keepers of the culture. They knew its history and secrets; they knew where to find healing plants and how to appease the gods and goddesses. Western and Christian influences have since marginalized the mahu in Hawaii.

EXPLORE FURTHER: *'O AU NO KEIA*

Read about the *mahu* and transgender communities of Hawaii in Andrew Matzner's *'O Au No Keia: Voices from Hawaii's Mahu and Transgender Communities* (Philadelphia: Xlibris, 2001). In his study, Matzner recorded oral narratives of some of Hawaii's contemporary male-to-female transgender persons. Each personal narrative begins with a photo of the speaker.

In Iran, where homosexuality is condemned by Islam and punished by lashing, transsexuals are gaining a level of acceptance with some Muslim clerics. In 1978, an early transsexual activist, Maryam Hatoon Molkara, who had previously been a man named Fereydoon, wrote a letter seeking religious guidance from the Ayatollah Ruhollah Khomeini. The ayatollah, who lived in exile at the time but later became the leader of the Islamic Revolution, replied that Molkara had his blessing as her case differed from that of a homosexual. Yet, when the revolution occurred in 1979, transgender and transsexual men were harassed, jailed, even tortured. Molkara was forbidden to continue dressing in women's clothes and was forced to take hormones to look like a man. The Islamic government repressed transgender people for many years, but now Muslim clerics who dominate the judiciary are better informed and more accepting; some even recommend sexual reassignment surgery where they feel it is warranted. Even with supportive clerics, transgender people face numerous obstacles in the male-dominated society where many cannot understand why a man of social standing would seek to become a woman of a lower social status. In Iran, the process of obtaining the proper documents for surgery and a new birth certificate is lengthy, requires the surgical candidate to carry a medical diagnosis of "Gender Identity Disorder," and is expensive, much as it is in the United States.[17]

In the traditionally patriarchal society of rural Albania and some parts of Bosnia and southern Serbia, where gender roles are inflexible, the practice of becoming "sworn virgins" is rooted in laws that date back to the fifteenth century. By traditional law, only men could own property and wives would become the husband's property upon marriage; however, becoming a sworn virgin allows a woman to live her life as a man, with the rights and privileges of a man. This is an important social role for families that do not have enough able-bodied men for the family to survive economically. Sworn virgins remain celibate throughout their lifetime, as the culture only recognizes traditional heterosexual relations. Life in the rural north is far removed from the bustling Albanian capital of Tirana, where

**EXPLORE FURTHER:
WOMEN WHO BECOME MEN**

Read about the sworn virgins of Eastern Europe in Antonia Young's *Women Who Become Men: Albanian Sworn Virgins (Dress, Body, Culture)* (Oxford: Berg, 2000). The National Geographic Channel followed Young in Albania for a segment of "Sexuality," a 2002 episode of the channel's series *Taboo.*

women are becoming independent in such areas as their choice of career; here, the phrase *sworn virgin* is dimly recognized but has little meaning.[18]

Given the myriad of social changes the world community weathered in the twentieth century, the undercurrent of societal tension as the new millennium approached is understandable. Amid a flurry of media hype, messages of gloom and doom were broadcast. The "millennium bug" was said to be lying dormant in the world's computers, set to awake with the dawning of the new century. The forecast was grim. The bug could shut down our now-computerized society, causing home computers to crash and disabling networked systems the world over. Everything from transportation to power stations and hospital equipment could be disabled, and people were urged to be prepared.

BEYOND THE YEAR 2000

Needless to say, the millennium bug did not cause the world's computers to simultaneously crash. Traffic did not come to a standstill; life support systems continued supporting life. Some of us who had begun to wonder if such a disaster was really possible may even have felt a little foolish. Lives continued without disruption, as did societal change.

The popularity of reality television shows in the twenty-first century has altered the face of American TV. The Bravo channel's smash hit *Queer Eye for the Straight Guy* has given millions of viewers opportunities to appreciate the artistic and aesthetic sensibilities from which gay male stereotypes have grown. In *Queer Eye*, whose tag line is "Five gay men, out to make over the world—one straight guy at a time" and which premiered in 2003, the campy and energetic team prides itself on turning one heterosexual male into a well-dressed, stylish, and cultured gentleman living in neat and attractive surroundings, within a sixty-minute time frame. The British version of the show premiered in 2004, starring another five gay men and a dog named Lulu; it aims to "improve a straight guy by helping him with Fashion, Food and Wine, Interior

Design, Culture and Grooming."[19] In a society that allows its straight men to be made over by gay men, can a reality show with transgender stars be far behind?

In 2005, the Sundance Channel premiered "TransGeneration," an original documentary series that follows four transgender college students as they transition on campus. Both the premiere and concluding episodes run an hour each, with the remaining six episodes running 30 minutes each. "TransGeneration" stars two male-to-female characters, Raci and Gabbie, and two female-to-male characters, T. J. and Lucas. Over the course of the series, each character explains his or her own personal struggle to find the appropriate gender identity and how family, friends, and the medical community fit into their lives. Directed by Jeremy Simmons and rated TV-14 for mild violence, adult language, and adult content, "TransGeneration" allows the viewing public to glimpse some aspects of life for transgender youth at college.

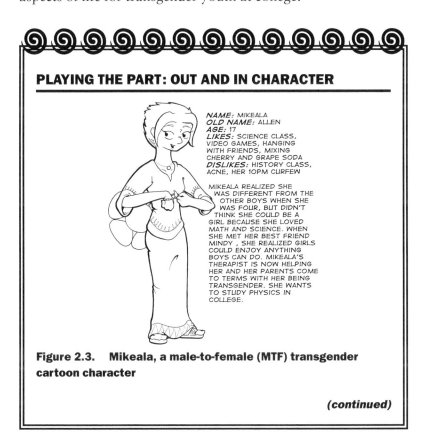

PLAYING THE PART: OUT AND IN CHARACTER

NAME: MIKEALA
OLD NAME: ALLEN
AGE: 17
LIKES: SCIENCE CLASS, VIDEO GAMES, HANGING WITH FRIENDS, MIXING CHERRY AND GRAPE SODA
DISLIKES: HISTORY CLASS, ACNE, HER 10PM CURFEW

MIKEALA REALIZED SHE WAS DIFFERENT FROM THE OTHER BOYS WHEN SHE WAS FOUR, BUT DIDN'T THINK SHE COULD BE A GIRL BECAUSE SHE LOVED MATH AND SCIENCE. WHEN SHE MET HER BEST FRIEND MINDY, SHE REALIZED GIRLS COULD ENJOY ANYTHING BOYS CAN DO. MIKEALA'S THERAPIST IS NOW HELPING HER AND HER PARENTS COME TO TERMS WITH HER BEING TRANSGENDER. SHE WANTS TO STUDY PHYSICS IN COLLEGE.

Figure 2.3.   Mikeala, a male-to-female (MTF) transgender cartoon character

(continued)

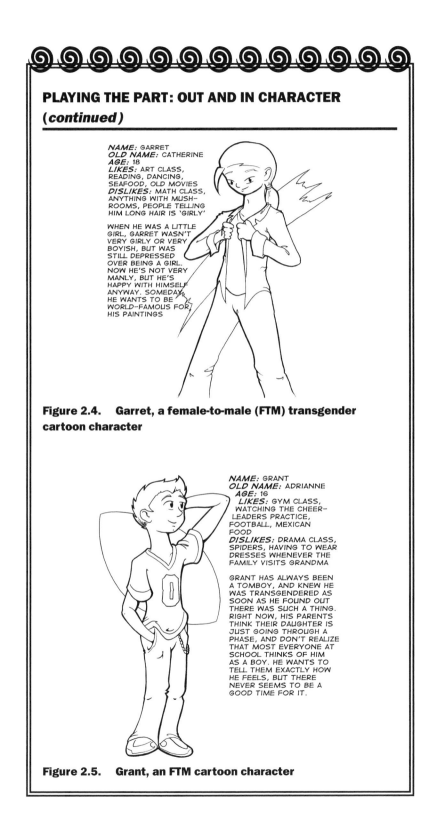

PLAYING THE PART: OUT AND IN CHARACTER
(*continued*)

NAME: GARRET
OLD NAME: CATHERINE
AGE: 18
LIKES: ART CLASS, READING, DANCING, SEAFOOD, OLD MOVIES
DISLIKES: MATH CLASS, ANYTHING WITH MUSHROOMS, PEOPLE TELLING HIM LONG HAIR IS 'GIRLY'

WHEN HE WAS A LITTLE GIRL, GARRET WASN'T VERY GIRLY OR VERY BOYISH, BUT WAS STILL DEPRESSED OVER BEING A GIRL. NOW HE'S NOT VERY MANLY, BUT HE'S HAPPY WITH HIMSELF ANYWAY. SOMEDAY, HE WANTS TO BE WORLD-FAMOUS FOR HIS PAINTINGS

Figure 2.4.   Garret, a female-to-male (FTM) transgender cartoon character

NAME: GRANT
OLD NAME: ADRIANNE
AGE: 16
LIKES: GYM CLASS, WATCHING THE CHEERLEADERS PRACTICE, FOOTBALL, MEXICAN FOOD
DISLIKES: DRAMA CLASS, SPIDERS, HAVING TO WEAR DRESSES WHENEVER THE FAMILY VISITS GRANDMA

GRANT HAS ALWAYS BEEN A TOMBOY, AND KNEW HE WAS TRANSGENDERED AS SOON AS HE FOUND OUT THERE WAS SUCH A THING. RIGHT NOW, HIS PARENTS THINK THEIR DAUGHTER IS JUST GOING THROUGH A PHASE, AND DON'T REALIZE THAT MOST EVERYONE AT SCHOOL THINKS OF HIM AS A BOY. HE WANTS TO TELL THEM EXACTLY HOW HE FEELS, BUT THERE NEVER SEEMS TO BE A GOOD TIME FOR IT.

Figure 2.5.   Grant, an FTM cartoon character

PLAYING THE PART: OUT AND IN CHARACTER
(*continued*)

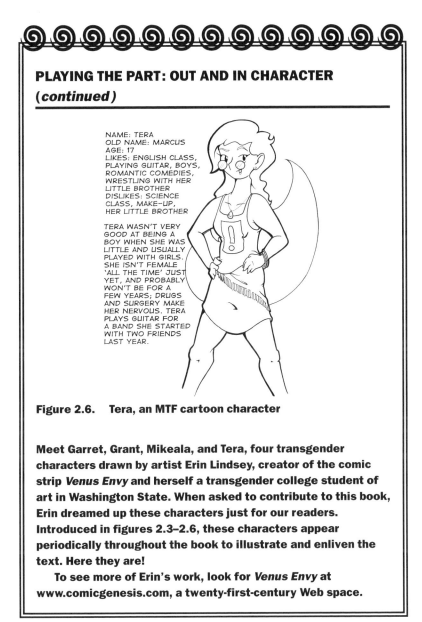

NAME: TERA
OLD NAME: MARCUS
AGE: 17
LIKES: ENGLISH CLASS,
PLAYING GUITAR, BOYS,
ROMANTIC COMEDIES,
WRESTLING WITH HER
LITTLE BROTHER
DISLIKES: SCIENCE
CLASS, MAKE-UP,
HER LITTLE BROTHER

TERA WASN'T VERY
GOOD AT BEING A
BOY WHEN SHE WAS
LITTLE AND USUALLY
PLAYED WITH GIRLS.
SHE ISN'T FEMALE
'ALL THE TIME' JUST
YET, AND PROBABLY
WON'T BE FOR A
FEW YEARS; DRUGS
AND SURGERY MAKE
HER NERVOUS. TERA
PLAYS GUITAR FOR
A BAND SHE STARTED
WITH TWO FRIENDS
LAST YEAR.

Figure 2.6.   Tera, an MTF cartoon character

Meet Garret, Grant, Mikeala, and Tera, four transgender characters drawn by artist Erin Lindsey, creator of the comic strip *Venus Envy* and herself a transgender college student of art in Washington State. When asked to contribute to this book, Erin dreamed up these characters just for our readers. Introduced in figures 2.3–2.6, these characters appear periodically throughout the book to illustrate and enliven the text. Here they are!

To see more of Erin's work, look for *Venus Envy* at www.comicgenesis.com, a twenty-first-century Web space.

In the present day across the United States, gender bending is visible on high school and college campuses, and gender blending can be found in towns and cities, stores and libraries. Yet, as normal as this appears to some of America, many people are not yet accepting. In fact, hate crimes are committed routinely against the gay/lesbian/bisexual/transgender (GLBT) community, and the most vicious attacks are often directed at transgender people. According to the National Transgender Advocacy Coalition (NTAC) website, gender intolerance was responsible for 264 deaths between 1970 and mid-2003.[20] By mid-December 2005, the Remembering Our Dead memorial website, the source for NTAC's figures, listed 353 names on the updated page.[21]

IN MEMORIAM: TRANSGENDER DAY OF REMEMBRANCE

The Transgender Day of Remembrance began as a candlelight vigil in San Francisco in 1999. Now observed annually on November 20 in major cities around the world, the day allows people to remember and honor the transgender victims lost to senseless, often brutal, violence in the prior year. To find locations for the current year's celebrations, visit www.gender.org.

TRANS PEOPLE AND GAY LIBERATION

In 1949, Dr. D. O. Cauldwell coined the word *transsexualism*, but it was Dr. Harry S. Benjamin, a New York sexologist and endocrinologist, who popularized the word. When Benjamin's book *The Transsexual Phenomenon* was published in 1966, few medical professionals had experience working with transsexualism. Benjamin and his colleague Wardell Pomeroy categorized transvestites separately from transsexuals. Further, Benjamin treated his transsexual patients with hormone therapy to help bring their bodies in line with their gender identities. In 1969 he was recognized as the "grandfather of transsexualism" and honored for his work in the field through the naming of the Harry Benjamin International Gender Dysphoria Association.[22]

Also in 1969, the Stonewall Riots in New York's Greenwich Village marked the birth of gay activism. Before that, GLBT rights were not taken seriously. Homosexual and transgender individuals were oppressed and marginalized by mainstream society. The riots began on June 27, 1969, when police raided the Stonewall Bar, a gay bar. This time, the patrons did not go quietly; they fought back! When the Tactical Patrol Force arrived, marching together to break up the crowd, it was greeted by a kick-dancing chorus line of transvestites singing, "We are the Stonewall Girls, we wear our hair in curls, . . ."—a surprising sight. The rioting continued for several nights, as increasing numbers of protesters arrived to add their voices to the fray. From this revolution, the Gay Liberation Front was born.

Although the Stonewall Girls may have kicked off gay liberation efforts, gains in gay rights do not necessarily include similar gains for transgender persons. For example in 2004, when same-sex marriage was legalized in the state of Massachusetts, a huge victory was won for the GLBT community as a whole, but the impact upon the trans community specifically was negligible. Still, the gay and trans communities continue to unite for the benefit of either or both groups. In 2005, the first Trans Day of Action for Social and Economic Justice March was held in New York to benefit transgender and gender non-conforming (TGNC) people who frequently face discrimination in the workplace and in general society. Originated by TransJustice of the Audre Lorde Project and "endorsed by the vast majority of national lesbian, gay, bi and trans organizations, as well as immigrant-rights, anti-police-brutality and racial-justice organizations,"[23] the June 24 march was timed to kick off the annual Gay Pride celebration. A crowd of 1,000 participants was reported to have demonstrated in the march, which concluded with a rally in New York's Union Square.

BE AWARE

Ask yourself: In failing to recognize trans people in history, or in underreporting the contributions of gay/lesbian/bisexual people, does our educational system discriminate against this marginalized segment of our society? As you learn more about underreported persons or groups—gay/lesbian/bisexual/transgender/intersex (GLBTI), Native American, anyone of non-European descent—consider sharing your knowledge when the situation allows. You can help to create a better-informed society.

Stay tuned for news of future events as the TGNC and GLBT communities continue to support the Gay Liberation movement. Events that don't make the mainstream media can be readily found online. (See the Resources section at the end of this book.)

NOTES

1. This paragraph draws from Joyce Tyldesley's biography *Hatchepsut: The Female Pharaoh* (New York: Viking, 1996).

2. *The Trial of Joan of Arc: Being the Verbatim Report of the Proceedings from the Orleans Manuscript*, translated by W. S. Scott (Westport, Conn.: Associated Booksellers, 1956), quoted in Leslie Feinberg, *Transgender Warriors: Making History from Joan of Arc to Dennis Rodman* (Boston: Beacon Press, 1996), 37.

3. This section draws extensively from "Highlights in Transgender History," in Lambda Legal Defense and Education Fund, "Bending the Mold: An Action Kit for Transgender Youth," www.lambdalegal.org/cgi-bin/iowa/documents/record?record=1504.

4. Vanessa Baird, *The No-Nonsense Guide to Sexual Diversity* (Toronto: New Internationalist Publications and Between the Lines, 2001), 121.

5. Baird, *No-Nonsense Guide to Sexual Diversity*, 114.

6. This section draws extensively from "Gender Benders," a 2004 episode of the National Geographic Channel series *Taboo*. See also "Aruvani—A Day in the Sun," a compilation of three BBC articles from 2001–2003, WE News Archive, www.thewe.cc/contents/more/archive/eunuch.html.

7. Kate Bornstein, *Gender Outlaw: On Men, Women, and the Rest of Us* (New York: Routledge, 1994), 23.

8. Ibid.

9. Lambda Legal Defense and Education Fund, "Bending the Mold."

10. Walter Williams, *The Spirit and the Flesh: Sexual Diversity in American Indian Culture* (Boston: Beacon Press, 1986), 178–81.

11. Feinberg, *Transgender Warriors*, 21.

12. Danny Lee, "The Pink Triangle: The Nazi Persecution of Gays," www.channel4.com/history/microsites/H/history/n-s/pink.html.

13. Susan Stryker, introduction to *Christine Jorgensen: A Personal Autobiography* (San Francisco: Cleis Press, 2001), reprinted in *Transgender Tapestry* 100 (Winter 2002): 25–26.

14. Gypsey Teague, "The Increase of Transgender Characters in Movies and Television," *Transgender Tapestry* 102 (Summer 2002): 31.

15. Walter Scott, "Personality Parade," *Parade*, 8 August 2004.

16. Andrew Matzner, *'O Au No Keia: Voices from Hawaii's Mahu and Transgender Communities* (Philadelphia: Xlibris, 2001), 42.

17. This paragraph draws extensively from Nazila Fathi, "As Repression Eases, More Iranians Change Their Sex," *New York Times*, 2 August 2004.

18. This paragraph draws extensively from "Sexuality," a 2002 episode of the National Geographic Channel series *Taboo*.

19. TV.com, *Queer Eye for the Straight Guy (UK)*, www.tv.com/queer-eye-for-the-straight-guy-uk/show/27996/summary.html.

20. Monica Helms, "Transgender Death Statistics," www.ntac.org.

21. Gwendolyn Ann Smith, "Remembering Our Dead," www.rememberingourdead.org/about/core.html.

22. Mildred L. Brown and Chloe Ann Rounsley, *True Selves: Understanding Transsexualism . . . for Families, Friends, Coworkers, and Helping Professionals* (San Francisco: Jossey-Bass, 1996), 29.

23. LeiLani Dowell, "First Trans Day of Action Draws 1,000," *Workers World*, 29 June 2005, www.workers.org/2005/us/trans-day-0707.

Terminology: What Do All Those Words Mean?

Although you'll find a glossary in the back of this book, this chapter examines language a bit more closely. Language is a powerful and fascinating tool. Ever changing, language responds to the knowledge and needs of its users. For example, peoples inhabiting Arctic regions have, and use, more words for "snow" than those of us living closer to the equator can possibly comprehend. Why? Because the experience of precipitation in such climates is far more complex than elsewhere. I grew up in New England. It wasn't until I was an adult that I understood that some of my Southern counterparts—while they understood *rain* and *snow*—were confused by the more specific terms such as *freezing rain*, *sleet*, or *black ice*. I discovered that my comprehension of these weather-related phenomena was more developed because my experience with them was greater. Once I understood that, it made more sense to me that people in Alaska have many more words for ice and snow than I know.

Keeping this in mind, it makes sense that people who have greater experience with variations of gender will have a vocabulary that goes beyond "he" and "she," "tomboy" and "sissy," or even California governor Arnold Schwarzenegger's oft-quoted "girlie men." As we explore language, keep in mind that some words carry with them emotional aspects and that some words can be perceived as hurtful—even when the speaker has no intention to hurt.

Where to begin, then? How about with pronouns?

MASTERING THE LINGO CAN BE TRICKY
Figure 3.1.   Garret consults a dictionary.

PRONOUNS

We're all familiar with the masculine and feminine pronouns *he* and *she*, *his* and *hers*. What happens when someone defies these boy–girl boundaries? Just as the feminist movement, denouncing the use of the term *men* to mean "both men and women," promoted a shift from, for example, *chairman* (or *chairwoman*) to *chairperson*, some persons in the trans community prefer the gender-neutral pronouns *hir* and *ze* (sometimes *zee* or *xe*). *Hir* is a gender-neutral replacement for *her* and *his*, and *ze* is a gender-neutral replacement for *he* and *she*. Leslie Feinberg, author of *Transgender Warriors: Making History from Joan of Arc to Dennis Rodman* (1996), credits the Internet as being the birthplace of these two words. Less than a decade later, I had a friend who went away to college and returned with these pronouns as part of hir working vocabulary. While *hir* and *ze* have not worked their way into my everyday vocabulary, I am aware of their existence and less likely to be stumped when encountering one of them. (Also, they will be useful in this chapter.)

The feminist movement can also be credited with the idea of replacing the purportedly male-identified word *history* with *her-story* . Feinberg invokes the trans liberation movement when taking the change or correction a step further—to *our-story*.

PREFIXES

Clearly, much meaning can be derived from a simple choice of prefix. Whereas *homo-* means "the same" or "equal," *hetero-* indicates "other" or "different." Thus, a homosexual is primarily interested, sexually, in his, her, or hir own gender, while a heterosexual is primarily interested, sexually, in a partner of another or a different sex. The prefix *bi-* indicates "two," so a bisexual is interested in partners of both sexes. In a world where the boy/girl dichotomy rules, one might imagine these three prefixes could pretty well cover the possibilities when paired with *sexual* to refer to interest in sexual partners. Not so. Indeed, some humans are *omnisexual*, sexually interested in any partner (from *omni-* meaning "all"). And, while *asexual* is generally used as a biology term to indicate the absence of reproductive sexuality, when a person calls him-, her-, or hirself *asexual*, the speaker probably means that he, she, or ze has no interest in sexual coupling whatsoever; the asexual are sexually disinterested.

When the above prefixes are connected with *sexual*, they refer to one's interest in or choice of sexual companion or partner. The prefixes *inter-* or *trans-* paired with *sexual*, on the other hand, refer to one's biological sex or the shape of one's genitals. The prefix *inter-* indicates being between or among something. For instance, you're familiar with *interstate*. The interstate highway system runs between and among states; it includes more than one state. Similarly, an *intersexual* has a body residing between male and female; it includes more than one sex.

Conversely, the prefix *trans-* before a noun indicates that it is across, beyond, or on the other side of where it began. Sticking with the travel analogy, a transcontinental flight or train trip is one that crosses a continent. *Transsexual* refers to one's biological sex as crossing from what one was (or is) to what one is (or wishes to be). Thus "trans" or "crossing" sexual lines covers a wealth of differences. Although some people try to simplify matters by using *transgender* for a person who feels he or she is of the sex opposite to the one assigned him or her at birth and *transsexual* for one who has undergone surgery, the language is far murkier than that. Someone who has male genitalia but feels female inside, yet has no intention of making a surgical change, or any change for that matter, may call themselves "transsexual," for such a person does cross the lines of sexual identity. To determine how any person wishes to be identified, listen closely to how that person identifies hirself, then model your language to the occasion. Other terms beginning to appear more frequently include the formal *gender nonconforming* and the informal *gender queer* for persons who do not identify as transgender or transsexual, but who push the limits of expected gender expression.

In the trans community, words such as *transman* or *transwoman* may be used to indicate someone who has crossed into a male or female identity. The poem in chapter 5 was written by someone who asked to be identified as a *tranny boy*. It can also appear as one word, or with boy spelled *boi*. Not limited to trans culture, *boi* appears to be working its way into mainstream culture. In the June/July 2004 *Jane* magazine, bois are listed as one of "six types of guys" that are recommended to women seeking dates.[1] That issue of *Jane* also includes a

> **TOPNOTCH RESOURCE: THE *OXFORD ENGLISH DICTIONARY***
>
> Although the standard for dictionaries is always the *Oxford English Dictionary*, the many specialty dictionaries available today provide more detailed excursions into the world of words. For greater understanding about the terminology discussed in this chapter, consult *Wimmin, Wimps and Wallflowers: An Encyclopædic Dictionary of Gender and Sexual Orientation Bias in the United States* by Philip H. Herbst, published in 2001 by the Intercultural Press, with a foreword by Morris Dees of the Southern Poverty Law Center. Herbst delves into the cultural history and usage of a vast collection of salient words.

personal essay titled "My Boyfriend Used to Be My Girlfriend" in its "It Happened to Me" column. Beyond simply the language, awareness of the trans community is gradually filtering into mainstream culture.

SUFFIXES

Beyond the impact of various prefixes on the words they modify, words can be equally impacted by the addition of a suffix. Since an important aspect of transgender or transsexual life may include surgical changes to the body, one cannot overlook the suffixes *-ectomy* and *-plasty*.

The suffix *-ectomy* indicates the removal of some part of the body through surgery. When a *tonsillectomy* is performed, a person's tonsils are removed. *Hysterectomy* refers to the removal of female sex organs. Transsexual surgery may include the removal of some body part(s).

It may also include the creation of body part(s). The suffix *-plasty* is related to *plastic*, meaning "malleable," and indicates formation or creation of some part of a body through surgery. When undergoing transsexual surgery, the body changes from one biological sex to another. In *vaginoplasty*, a vagina is constructed where one did not exist previously. Similarly, *phalloplasty* indicates surgical construction of a penis. More information about surgical changes appears in chapter 7, "Transformations."

ACRONYMS

Acronyms—abbreviations formed using selected letters or parts of words from other words or phrases and then used as words themselves—abound in today's world, and they can be confusing. Indeed, long acronyms that do not form pronounceable words are sometimes disparagingly referred to as "alphabet soup." On the other hand, acronyms make lengthy oft-repeated names or phrases much simpler for speakers, writers, and readers. An acronym communicates a whole chunk of information in a shorter form.

The acronym GSA, short for "gay–straight alliance," is commonly heard on many high school and college campuses. The concept of a gay–straight alliance was developed before someone thought to make the name more inclusive. Today, gay–straight–bisexual alliance groups can be found, but in general the acronym GSA is still used, referring to a group of people of varying sexual orientations and gender preferences banding together with straight allies to discuss issues of sexuality and gender. An important aspect of GSAs is the inclusive nature of the group; one need not have any specific sexual orientation or gender identity or expression to join a GSA.

Imagine joining the GLBTQSIQA. Now, that's a mouthful worthy of the nickname alphabet soup. The gay–lesbian–bisexual–transgender–queer–straight–intersex–questioning alliance may hold meetings as frequently as the simpler GSA; however, one might understand if a school administration or university radio station balked at making as frequent public service announcements for the GLBTQSIQA as for the simpler-to-pronounce GSA. Then again, dropping the words *straight* and *alliance*, the acronyms GLBT, LGBT, LGBTQ, LGBTI, or even LGBTQQ are seen more and more frequently as speakers seek to be inclusive of all minority sexual orientations and gender identities. The *gay and lesbian* or *lesbian and gay* beginnings of such acronyms are nearly interchangeable—which means that when one is in the process of creating a name they are transposable. Once an organization has decided upon its name, though, the pieces are no longer moveable; the order is set. Although both transsexual and transgender are often included in such names, I have not encountered more than one *T* in these acronyms, but interestingly enough a second *Q* may be added to include both *questioning* as well as *queer-identified* persons. Also, sometimes an *I* is used to represent intersex individuals. The inclusive form used today, LGBTQQ—for lesbian, gay, bisexual, transgender (and/or transsexual), queer, and questioning—may itself be outdated by the time you're reading this book. What is important is to understand what each letter of this evolving acronym represents. Indeed, the first TransJustice Day of Action in 2005 sought to unite the LGBT community to address TGNC issues, that is, issues of trans and gender nonconforming persons. Stay tuned!

Much simpler are the acronyms indicating a gender change. When a biologically male person presents as a female, hir gender change is male-to-female, represented by the acronym MTF. Similarly, the genetic female who presents as a male is called female-to-male (FTM). Throughout this text, readers will encounter both of these acronyms.

When perusing the Resources section at the end of this book, readers will encounter acronyms following the names of many organizations. Acronyms are to phrases or organization names what instant messaging (yes, IMing) is to written communication. Those of us who still prize the postal letter find that occasions for using it are diminishing as technology becomes fully integrated in our daily lives.

PHOBIAS

As difficult as this may be for some readers to believe, many people (especially older adults) have yet to experience instant messaging. While a generation lives with it, those who continue to be unfamiliar with IMing may also be leery of it. For people raised when computers were a rarity, the reasons for not using instant messaging essentially boil down to one: fear of the unknown. Fear, however disguised, hinders progress into the technological age. Such fear-based roadblocks are common elements of human behavior.

Fears, large and small, can often be allayed with education; however, fear itself often stands in the way of education. *The*

New Shorter Oxford English Dictionary (1993) defines *phobia* as "(A) fear, (a) horror, (an) aversion; especially an abnormal or irrational fear or dread aroused by a particular object or circumstance" and defines the suffix *-phobia* as "denoting (especially irrational) fear, dislike, [or] antipathy." Note that both definitions hinge upon the use of the word *irrational*. That's where education comes in.

In *Families Like Mine* (2004), author Abigail Garner takes the word *homophobia*, fear of homosexual people, to another level by identifying two levels of homophobia.[2] According to Garner, homophobes (people with homophobia) are either "homo-hesitant" or "homo-hostile," which is an important distinction. Homo-hesitant people are unsure about where they stand on gay issues, probably because they are uninformed about them. These people, when educated, could become allies for the gay community—or not. Homo-hesitant people may overcome their hesitancy simply by learning more about gays, perhaps by realizing that many people they already know and accept are gay. Homo-hostile people, on the other hand, have a strong dislike of or even revulsion toward gay people. These people can be dangerous to be around for people who are gay— or even for people the homo-hostile people *perceive* to be gay. Homo-hostile people murdered Teena Brandon, Matthew Shepard, Gwen Arujo, and many others. They often feel justified in their disdain for people who are not "natural" or "normal," which includes LGBTQ people in the eyes of the homo-hostile person, and they seem to have no trouble using slurs or derogatory language to describe those whom they disdain.

DEROGATORY OR PEJORATIVE WORDS

Language used to hurt others, or derogatory language, twists the meaning of a word to make it pejorative. For example, when I refer to the gay community, meaning the GLBTQ community, I am making a positive reference, but someone who sneers, "That's so gay!" is slurring the meaning of the word. Even though the speaker, when confronted, may deny intent to hurt homosexuals or the people who care about them, allowing even casually spoken slurs to go unchallenged sends a message of acceptance for such language and attitudes. While it may seem like a minor issue, voicing objections to such intolerant language is one step in the path to reducing antigay or gender-biased violence.

Speaking out against pejorative language need not be a drawn-out, complicated affair. By simply informing a speaker that the pejorative language has been heard and is not appreciated, one makes a speaker aware that "That's so gay!" might be a phrase nearing time for retirement. Responses as plain as "Don't say that," "That's not cool," or "I don't appreciate it when you say that" can alert a speaker that his or her language is not acceptable.

Just about any word can be used in a pejorative manner. Tone of voice conveys as much information as a word itself—sometimes more. Words that are meant to hurt, such as *faggot*, *queer*, and *dyke*, can be adopted by the group they were initially intended to hurt. This is called "taking back the language," when the targeted group takes ownership of and pride in the words. An excellent example of this appears in the

BE AWARE

The Gay–Straight Alliance (GSA) Network, an organization within the California school system, provides a publication entitled *Take It Back* to help students combat derogatory language and slurs through student organizing and activism on their campuses. The manual begins by examining and analyzing the history of the power structures behind common campus slurs, and it includes statistics about slurs and harassment. It also includes campaign strategies for educating peers, teachers, and administrators. A section of sample materials consists of a student survey, lesson plans for working with separate peer and teacher groups in the form of workshop agendas, and two workshop handouts. For people interested in changing campus climates, this sixty-page manual provides a good start.

title story of the 1994 young adult anthology *Am I Blue?* edited by Marion Dane Bauer. The story "Am I Blue?" written by Bruce Coville, features a character named Melvin who was the victim of a fatal gay-bashing incident and is now working in the role of fairy godfather. At one point Melvin explains how he landed his current job saying, "'I didn't want to be anyone's guardian angel . . . [and] people had been calling me a fairy all my life, and now that I was dead, that was what I wanted to be.'" Melvin does more than take back the language for a one-time use—he assumes it as his identity and employment.

SYMBOLS

Symbols, or logos, use an image to represent an idea. Just as acronyms use letters to represent a phrase, visual symbols use images to convey a concept. Think of the Nike logo, that simple quasi-checkmark that represents a huge company, its products, and even says something about the people who use them. The gay community also employs images to convey ideas. For example, it adopted the rainbow to represent inclusion of diversity. Of course, other groups also use rainbow flags. The Rainbow Coalition uses the rainbow, as does the peace movement with the rainbow peace flag. The concept of accepting and celebrating diversity is embraced by a number of movements.

In Nazi Germany during World War II, symbols were used to label undesirable people. In addition to tattooing numbers on their prisoners' forearms, the Nazis began by writing labels on their prisoners in concentration camps. At first, entering Jews were labeled *Juden* (Jew), while homosexuals had "Paragraph 175" (referring to the German penal code) written on their backs. Soon the Nazis realized that using symbols to label prisoners was much simpler. Jews were made to wear a yellow Star of David, and homosexuals were forced to wear pink triangles. Since pedophiles and other sex offenders were also labeled with the pink triangle, this symbol led viewers to associate its wearer with the commission of sexual perversions.[3] Sometime after the war, the pink triangle was adopted as a

**Figure 3.2.
Transgender symbol**

symbol by the gay community. Today pink triangle stickers, buttons, and even jewelry are worn to symbolize gay pride.

Although the pink triangle represents the gay community, the logo in figure 3.2 was created specifically to represent the transgender community. Made by trans activist Nancy Nangeroni—from a drawing by activist Holly Boswell in North Carolina—the transgender symbol is highly visible on the Internet today and is recognized worldwide. Linking the internationally accepted symbols for male ♂ and female ♀ together with a new symbol that combines the two to represent transgender, Nangeroni softened all the edges, added color, and created a pin. In her posting on the GenderTalk website, Nangeroni explains her reasoning: "I made it of soft shapes to connote gentility, accommodation, and permission. I placed it on a lavender triangle [because] it's time we, the crossdressing–transsexual–transgender community, took a stand in support of the gay community." Atop the lavender triangle, the bright blue symbol represents strength. After mounting this colorful symbol on a pin, she donated the symbol to the community, and requests "that we make it stand for honor & integrity, compassion for all, and good humor." Nangeroni no longer produces the pins, but the symbol is in the public domain, which means you are free to use it yourself.[4]

TITLES OF ADDRESS

While visual symbols and logos symbolize concepts, and acronyms represent words and phrases, how many of us give thought to the titles by which we ourselves are addressed? One frequently overlooked aspect of interpersonal communication is the title with which one person addresses another. You probably address your physician as "Doctor" and a man with whom you are not on a first-name basis as "Mister." Men do not encounter issues with titles quite as often as do women. Except for those who have earned some other title such as "Doctor" or "Reverend," most women age twenty-something or beyond eventually encounter the issue of whether they wish to be addressed as "Miss," "Ms.," or "Mrs."

Forty years ago, during the civil rights movement but before the women's liberation movement had taken hold, the choices were simpler. When the choices were simply "Miss" or "Mrs.," one could size up the person being addressed (Was she wearing a wedding ring? Did she look old enough to be married?) and guess. Unmarried women would be addressed as "Miss," while married women became "Mrs.," a title generally followed by the husband's surname. Then women's liberation allowed women to protest the disparity between sexes. Why were men always "Mr.," a title that did not indicate marital status, but women were distinguished by marital status? The neutral *Ms.* entered our vocabulary, and women could choose to be addressed as "Ms.," a title which acknowledged their femininity but left their marital status unstated. With such a simple alternative, why don't we just address every female as "Ms." and sidestep the whole marital status issue? One reason is tradition.

Tradition is the usual, sometimes ritualistic, way we do things. (For example, it is traditional for stores to hold sales connected with holidays or certain times of the year. Can you imagine an August without a blizzard of back-to-school sales advertisements?) People hold onto traditions for all sorts of reasons. When a woman introduces herself as "Mrs.," some people address her as such, while others may use "Ms." or even "Miss." The reasons for this may include ignorance, inattention, sloppiness, or even misguided flattery—such as when the speaker uses "Miss" to imply youthfulness on the part of the addressee. Similar mistakes might include addressing a

PERSONAL EXPERIENCE: "NAMETAG," BY CAMILLE PERRI, GENDER-BENDING FEMALE, AGE 23

Reality. It's whatever you think it is. Luckily we can create our own realities, our own consciousness and build our own communities, and essentially, our own world. But every once in a while, like a baby forced from the womb, we must squint our eyes and step out of our own reality and into the mainstream. There we are reminded of how offensive the dominant reality is. It's the reality of a world made up of people who don't understand us, who fear us, and resent us for making them uncomfortable. In such a world we are cast as the enemy and fighting our way through isn't always so easy. I knew getting a *real* job was going to be a hard-fought battle.

I thought it was going to work out, that I would be able to successfully straddle that fine line of living an alternative lifestyle while working a conventional job without compromising who I am or what I believe in. After all, they did hire me in spite of my short bleached blond hair and I had gotten away with wearing my androgynous suits to work, if you could call that something to get away with. One doesn't usually think of being oneself as getting away with something. It makes it sound as if it was a theft or a murder or something sinister. But when you're a gender bender in mainstream America, you can be made to feel like a criminal, and in a sense you are. You're breaking the rules, rules you don't believe in that others have a great investment in upholding.

That reality first smacked me in the face on my third day on the job. It was on that day that I walked in to the mysterious yellow post-it note stuck to my desk with my boss' handwriting sprawled across it. It read: "What would you like your nametag to read? Miss Perri, Ms. Perri, or Camille Perri?" It appeared to be giving me a choice. It would have been nicer if "Mr." would have been a choice as well, but I knew that wasn't a realistic wish, and not necessarily one that would have been desirable to me anyway. I was glad that I was not going to be forced to use a title prefixed to my name that would define me as a woman and even worse, as a married or unmarried (in other words owned by a man or looking for a man to have me) woman.

I should have just circled "Camille Perri" on the note and quietly stuck it on my boss's desk and then made a clean

(continued)

PERSONAL EXPERIENCE: "NAMETAG," BY CAMILLE PERRI, GENDER-BENDING FEMALE, AGE 23 (*continued*)

getaway, but I didn't. I made the mistake of saying my choice aloud. Everyone in the room immediately surrounded me. They were shouting things at me like, "Oh no you don't, you don't want your full name for everyone to see, not with the sickos we get in here."

"If they want to find out my name, they will," I replied.

"It's not professional enough, you have to demand respect," they told me. "You don't want people calling you by your first name. You're not a kid anymore." To them I was a kid, younger than all of them by at least twenty years.

I tried to resist but they ganged up on me until finally one of them, the most wicked of the group, leaned down into my face like a vicious principal giving a student detention. She said to me, so close that the heat of her breath hit my face as she spoke, "Tell me, do you want to be an adult?" I pulled my head back but she leaned farther in, trapping me. Before I could answer she continued, "Are you ready to grow up?"

I let out a "no."

They found that humorous and scattered away amid jovial laughter. As far as they were concerned, I was joking and the issue had been resolved.

"It's not about being an adult," I said meekly, but my words were left hanging in the air to dissolve into nothingness. It was as if I hadn't said anything at all.

As they reprimanded me for not acting like a grownup, they made me feel like more of a child than ever. Like bad parents, they used their age and authority to bully me without granting me any agency or believing that I could be in disagreement with them and still be right. So, like the child they made of me, I whimpered away to my own corner—drowned in my own futility, lacking the vocabulary and the assertiveness to stand up to them and for myself.

"It's not about being an adult," I told them, but I couldn't go on, I couldn't finish my sentence. I couldn't say that it wasn't about being an adult but that it was about my gender. What if I had said those words? What would have happened? I would have gotten hot and turned red, but what would they have done? Would they have fallen silent? Would they have laughed harder? Would they have asked me to explain what I meant or would they have told me that that was childish, too? I know for

PERSONAL EXPERIENCE: "NAMETAG," BY CAMILLE PERRI, GENDER-BENDING FEMALE, AGE 23 (*continued*)

sure they wouldn't have understood, but how would they have reacted?

My nametag should be coming in a few days. I will have to wear the little golden tag that labels me "Ms. Perri" like a scarlet letter, which will burn a hole through my shirt and into my chest each day and remind me of the fear that kept me silent. I could also view it as an everyday reminder to get down on myself, to sink myself further each day into self-doubt and self-hatred. But that would be giving a little gold rectangle and a group of dried up old women way too much power over me. I'm not proud of backing down from them, but I forgive myself for it.

Each and every day is a battle when you're a gender outlaw, and even the strongest soldiers lose a battle once in a while. So I prefer to think of my nametag as a purple heart or a medal, honoring my courage but reminding me that it's ok to be human, too. Most importantly, it will remind me that the dominant reality is a harsh one, and it is a reality that can't be escaped. I will use this lesson to be better prepared for the next time my back is up against the wall and my gender being held hostage. Next time I will be ready.

Are you armed and ready for battle in what they call the "real world"?

young woman as "ma'am" or with the title "Mrs." when the speaker wishes to imply maturity on the part of the addressee.

For another perspective on names and titles of address, read the previous personal essay, "Nametag," by Camille Perri, a gender-bending twenty-three-year-old female.

When all angles are considered, language is far more powerful than "just words." Changing the beginning of a word, or the tone with which a word is voiced, may change the entire message being conveyed. Most of us, myself included, fail to give language the credit it deserves. By neglecting to use care with our word choices, we risk not only degrading the language but also inadvertently hurting others with poorly chosen words.

My mother always said, "Think before you speak."

To that I now say, "Yes, Mom, that's good advice. I'll try harder."

NOTES

1. Katy McColl, "Don't Lose Your Head Over That Normal Dude," *Jane*, June/July 2004, 142–45.

2. Abigail Garner, *Families Like Mine* (New York: HarperCollins, 2004).

3. Danny Lee, "The Pink Triangle: The Nazi Persecution of Gays," www.channel4.com/history/microsites/H/history/n-s/pink.html.

4. Nancy Nangeroni, "About the TG Symbol: Where Did It Come From?" GenderTalk, 2004, www.gendertalk.com/info/tgsymbol.shtml.

4

Boy or Girl? Delivery Room Decisions and Intersex Infants

HELPING PEOPLE UNDER-
STAND GENDER ISSUES
HELPS YOU, TOO

THE NEW ARRIVAL

When that long-awaited, much-anticipated event occurs in the delivery room, every parent wants to know right away, "Is it a boy or a girl?" Imagine yourself as a new parent asking this question. It could be answered in one of three ways. The first would be a direct answer—"It's a boy!" or "It's a girl!"—and your response would most likely be parental feelings of pride and joy. Now imagine a second scenario: your health care practitioner answers the question decisively, only to change the answer later. Certainly you would be anxious, but having received one of the standard answers (well, two now), you would likely be relieved. A third alternative exists: the health care practitioner answers, "I'm not sure," perhaps continuing, "It could be either (or both)." Imagine that! The doctor doesn't know?! Clearly, you would have preferred a clear either/or response.

In the vast majority of births, determining the biological sex of an infant is as simple as checking for the presence of a penis or a vagina. These are considered primary sex characteristics, and one of the distinct indicators of a person's sex. If the baby has a penis, it is declared male; if it has a vagina, it is female. In an extremely small number of cases, the delivery room staff may make the wrong determination. Unless the infant's legs are spread and a careful examination of the body is made, an enlarged clitoris or an absent scrotum could be cause for a mistaken declaration by a hasty medical practitioner.

The second scenario occurs across the United States when an infant is born with what is viewed as a deformity by some, which has resulted in some sort of sexual ambiguity. As many as 1 percent of babies may be born with genitals that do not fit the standard male or female, and about 1 percent of these babies will receive surgery to "normalize" their genital appearance (see chart later in this chapter). Maybe the baby had an enlarged clitoris, which the obstetrician identified as a penis and you had been told, "It's a boy!" only to have the proclamation changed upon the discovery of the infant's vagina. Maybe the baby had a micropenis, so small as to be mistaken for a clitoris, but after the announcement, "It's a girl!" no vagina was found. The medical practitioners may then go on to explain the confusion as a minor problem or malformation that they feel needs attention, and which can be resolved through genital surgery when the child is a few months older. When seen as a deformity, intersex conditions are treated as psychosocial emergencies—problems that affect the emotional and social well-being of the infant and the infant's family members. Parents are thought to need a definitive answer to the question of their child's sex because they will interact differently with a "boy" baby than with a "girl" baby. The work done by Dr. John Money and his research team, addressed in chapter 1, views intersex births in this manner.

The third scenario is also possible. Some health care practitioners may admit, while still in the delivery room, that the baby's sex is unclear. When the external genitalia are not clearly and entirely either male or female, their ambiguity causes confusion. In geographic areas with many medical professionals, such as cities with major teaching hospitals, teams may quickly be called in for consultation. Not all communities have such luxuries, though, and some children grow up with ambiguous genitals and without counseling. Some parents accept their baby as a child, rather than as a boy or a girl, and agree to an assignment of gender without allowing surgical intervention. With or without additional attention, the intersex child may receive a name common to either gender, such as "Leslie," or "Taylor," or "Chris," then be given the room to grow.

Figure 4.1.   Gender confusion can occur in the delivery room.

Realize that the term "intersex" is used to describe more conditions than simply ambiguous genitalia; read the next section on chromosomes and fetal development to understand. No matter the response to the question "What [sex] is it?" all parents definitely have a new baby in their lives, ready to be loved.

The view promoted by the Intersex Society of North America (ISNA) holds that no "corrective" action for ambiguous genitalia needs to be taken during infancy. Rather, the society advocates that the child be allowed to grow up with whatever ambiguity appeared at birth and that any surgical intervention be delayed until after the child has reached puberty—at which time the child should be allowed to determine his/her gender of choice. ISNA was formed by Cheryl

Chase who—distressed and angry at having been subjected to such surgery as an infant—chose to speak out as an advocate on behalf of intersex people to inform the medical community that intersexuals must navigate social stigma and trauma, and that intersexuality is not a problem of gender. Realizing that parents and health care professionals are often traumatized by dealing with a situation as unfamiliar as intersexuality, and that infant sex assignment is required legally and socially, ISNA advocates that gender be assigned without surgery and that surgical intervention only occur after the patient has become of age to participate actively in the decision-making process.[1] One reason for waiting is that beyond the identity issues, these genital surgeries can render patients sterile or rob them of sexual sensation. Also, related complications appearing in the patient's future could require additional surgery, hormone treatments, or other medical interventions.

Research studies at Johns Hopkins Children's Center in 2000 support ISNA's position. Dr. William Reiner, of the Child and Adolescent Psychiatry Clinic for Gender Identity and Psychosexual Disorders, and Dr. John Gearhart, director of pediatric urology, conducted separate studies with similar outcomes. Both show that nature, not nurture, supplies the deciding element of gender identity. Subsequently, Reiner has "called for a thorough reexamination of the practice of sex-reassignment of children, and urged extreme caution in surgically reconstructing these children at birth."[2] Such studies are made necessary by the number of babies born each year whose gender is not easily identified in the delivery room.

About one in every 2,000 babies born each year has genitals that are not clearly either male or female, but which look ambiguous—the baby could be of either sex, or be both sexes.[3] In addition, some people with genitalia that are clearly either male or female have chromosomal (genetic) anomalies and/or hormonal imbalances that create ambiguity. The American Educational Gender Information Service (AEGIS) website reports, "Since genetic testing was instituted for women in the Olympic Games, a number of women have been disqualified as 'not women' after winning. However, none of the disqualified

**TELEVISION SPECIAL:
"IS IT A BOY OR A GIRL?"**
The Discovery Channel aired a one-hour documentary on medical management of children with ambiguous sex anatomy titled "Is It a Boy or a Girl?" in 2000. The documentary addresses children born with mixed sex characteristics and the complexities of gender, beyond simply the shape of one's genitals. Produced by Ward & Associates and endorsed by ISNA, video (VHS) copies are currently available through ISNA.

women is a man."[4] Any one of several medical conditions may account for such ambiguities, but before exploring them, a review of the basics is in order.

CHROMOSOMES AND FETAL DEVELOPMENT

In general, humans have forty-six chromosomes in each of the cells in our bodies, twenty-three pairs. Twenty-two chromosomes and a sex chromosome (X) come from the mother and twenty-two others and either an X or a Y sex chromosome come from the father. A blood test called a *karyotype* is used to analyze chromosomal makeup. Most people's karyotype is either 46,XX (female) or 46,XY (male). When anomalies occur, the resulting baby is different somehow from most people. Down Syndrome, which has nothing to do with gender identity, is a well-known genetic anomaly where one of the two initial cells (either the egg or the sperm) has an extra twenty-first chromosome, resulting in the baby having 47, instead of 46, chromosomes in each of its cells. Some intersex conditions are just as common as Down Syndrome, but they remain nearly invisible in our society for cultural reasons.

At conception, the egg cell provides an X chromosome, and the sperm cell provides either a female-determining X chromosome or a male-determining Y chromosome. However, intersex conditions may occur, and a fertilized egg cell containing a Y chromosome can develop into a female or an intersexual. A specific gene on the Y chromosome has been identified as the sex-determining region of the Y chromosome (or SRY). If the Y chromosome is missing this SRY gene, the egg will develop into a female.[5] A developed male infant has a penis; a Wolffian duct, which connects to the gonads that have developed into testes; and XY sex chromosomes. In a developed female infant, the erectile tissue has developed into a clitoris; the Mullerian duct has differentiated into the vagina and uterus, the ovaries, and the fallopian tubes that connect them; and XX sex chromosomes.

Problems may develop while chromosomes, gonads, or genitals are taking shape. When chromosomes, gonads, and genitals are not all aligned as male or female, the child is intersex. Usually, though, only ambiguities in genital appearance trigger concern about intersexuality in the delivery room. A few of the possible intersex conditions are discussed below.

KLINEFELTER SYNDROME

One of the most common chromosomal variations in humans is Klinefelter Syndrome, which involves an extra X chromosome in males; this creates a hormonal imbalance in the body. Named for Dr. Harry Klinefelter because his name was listed first on a 1942 paper published about the condition, it is found once in about every 500 to 1,000 live born male infants. The genetic makeup of these males is generally 47,XXY although those with the less common variations of 48,XXXY; 48,XXYY;

TELEVISION SPECIAL: "GENDER: UNKNOWN"

On television, the Discovery Health Channel's *Medical Mysteries* series in 2000 aired an episode titled "Gender: Unknown" that portrayed the experiences of three persons "caught between male and female." Intersex children, it reported, have a driving need to understand not only who they are, but what they are. Each of the three stories is compelling.

Tammy, from Denver, a woman who has Androgen Insensitivity Syndrome, is genetically male but her anatomy is female. As a nursing student, one day in class she learned that her condition was called testicular feminization and that others have this condition. Only then did she realize that she could have been a man except for gonad-removal surgery she had undergone as a young teen. Today she struggles against osteoporosis because her body doesn't produce sufficient estrogen.

Max, a father in Atlanta, was born with genitals that are neither male or female. Doctors advised that he would be happier being raised as a girl, and he was named Judy. When he hit puberty and began to menstruate, doctors performed emergency surgery to create a vagina for him. As an adult he saw the diagnosis "male pseudohermaphrodite" in his medical records and went to the library to learn more. Later when he met his soul mate, she did not care that his body was different and supported his transition to male when he couldn't accept himself in a female body. Today they are happily married and have children.

Patrick is still a child. Since being adopted at birth, his parents have been strong advocates for his health care. He was born with a tiny penis, an internal ovary and fallopian tubes, and a single testicle. When Patrick was an infant, doctors wanted to operate to remove the minute penis, and his parents refused; they felt Patrick should play with other intersex children and decide about surgery when he was older. The doctors managed to get consent for another procedure—a diagnostic biopsy—and then performed the surgery that had been refused, telling the parents that the testicle was malignant and so needed to be removed. The medical team believed they were acting in the child's best interests, despite the wishes of the parents. But the pathology report described normal, healthy, testicle tissue. Now, Patrick is very small for his age, and too weak to keep up with his playmates. He takes growth hormone and will need to take testosterone later.

Tammy, Max, and Patrick lead normal lives in every way except that their physical genders differ from the norm.

49,XXXXY; and XY/XXY mosaic are also considered to have Klinefelter Syndrome. Diagnosable through a karyotype, or chromosome analysis, many males with the syndrome likely go undiagnosed because they exhibit no reason to be tested. The most common characteristics of Klinefelter Syndrome include sterility, breast development, incomplete masculine body build, and problems either socially or with school and learning. Treatment with testosterone in males who have low hormone levels is usually successful, except testosterone therapy cannot reverse the sterility. Even so, it may help some to realize that they are not alone in this, because infertility is a significant problem among couples today; it is estimated that one in ten couples are unable to conceive.[6]

EXPLORE FURTHER: KLINEFELTER SYNDROME

More information about Klinefelter Syndrome is available from Klinefelter Syndrome and Associates in Coto de Caza, California. Visit their website at http://genetic.org/ks.

TURNER SYNDROME

A chromosomal condition affecting girls only, Turner Syndrome occurs when one of the two X chromosomes normally found in females is absent or incomplete. Named for Dr. Henry Turner, who first described the condition's features in the late 1930s, Turner Syndrome is characterized most commonly by limited height and deficient ovarian development. Caused by the partly or completely missing X chromosome, Turner Syndrome seems to occur randomly. Although named in 1938, the chromosomal irregularity that is now used to make the specific diagnosis of Turner Syndrome was not discovered for another twenty-one years, when the technology to perform the blood test called a karyotype was available. Now diagnosable by this simple blood test, there is no "cure" for it as such, but the girls and women affected can live complete and fulfilling lives. Treatments may include the introduction of growth hormone to help patients achieve "normal" height and estrogen replacement therapy to aid in the development of secondary sexual characteristics.

Modern reproductive technologies have been used to help Turner Syndrome women become pregnant. Other problems, including conditions of the heart, thyroid, or kidneys, may require that the Turner Syndrome woman have good medical care throughout her life. About one in every 2,500 live female births is affected by the condition.[7]

EXPLORE FURTHER: TURNER SYNDROME SOCIETY

To learn more about Turner Syndrome, contact the Turner Syndrome Society of the United States in Houston, Texas. It's listed in the Resources section at the end of this book, under Organizations. The society has a toll-free phone number, a user-friendly website, and a variety of publications available for interested persons.

MAYER-ROKITANSKY-KUSTER-HAUSER SYNDROME

Mayer-Rokitansky-Kuster-Hauser Syndrome (abbreviated as MRKH or MRKHauser Syndrome), also known as Mullerian Agenesis or Vaginal Agenesis, is a congenital total or partial absence of the uterus or vagina. Occurring once in every 5,000–6,000 births, MRKH babies are typical XX females who are born with ovaries and

EXPLORE FURTHER: MAYER-ROKITANSKY-KUSTER-HAUSER SYNDROME SUPPORT GROUPS

More information and confidential support groups for MRKH women or the parents of an MRKH baby are available through the MRKH Organization at www.mrkh.org. Clinical information can be found at the Museum of Menstruation and Women's Health at www.mum.org.

typical external genitalia, but whose vagina, uterus, and fallopian tubes are incomplete or missing. Often born with the lower portion of the vagina intact, MRKH girls easily go undetected until puberty, when the absence of menstruation may alert medical practitioners to an irregularity.[8]

ANDROGEN INSENSITIVITY SYNDROME

Androgen Insensitivity Syndrome (AIS), Androgen Resistance Syndrome, and Testicular Feminization (TFM) are all different terms for the same condition, although the name Testicular Feminization is outdated (and offensive to some). Occurring in approximately one in 13,000–20,000 people, AIS is a recessive genetic defect occurring on the X chromosome; thus, AIS runs in families. With AIS, the body is unable to respond to androgen ("male" hormones). The level of androgen insensitivity varies between individuals. The three descriptors for AIS are Complete Androgen Insensitivity Syndrome (CAIS), Partial Androgen Insensitivity Syndrome (PAIS), and Mild Androgen Insensitivity Syndrome (MAIS).

CAIS babies are usually clearly female, although they may have undescended or partially descended testes, and the vagina is usually both short and without a cervix. As women, breasts do develop, but menstruation does not occur. The secrecy surrounding their condition can make children and women with AIS feel more of the emotional strain of being different. (On the Discovery Health Channel production "Gender: Unknown," aired in 2000, one of the subjects followed, Tammy, shares her experience with having this condition.) PAIS babies can be one of three phenotypes (observable anatomies): predominately female, ambiguous, or predominately male. MAIS babies are clearly male at birth but may experience breast development (gynecomastia) at puberty.

EXPLORE FURTHER: ANDROGEN INSENSITIVITY SYNDROME SUPPORT GROUP

More information is available through the Androgen Insensitivity Syndrome Support Group (AISSG) at www.medhelp.org/www/ais.

PROGESTIN-INDUCED VIRILIZATION

An XX (female) fetus exposed to androgens—such as progestin, which was used in the 1950s and 1960s to prevent miscarriage—can be born with observable sexual characteristics ranging from "female with larger clitoris" to "male with no testes." Ovaries and a uterus do develop, although in some extreme cases the vagina and cervix may be absent. Occasionally, such children are assigned male identities and raised as boys. In all cases, ISNA recommends that the child be informed about her biology and that she not be prematurely subjected to cosmetic genital surgery.[9]

5-ALPHA REDUCTASE DEFICIENCY

5-alpha reductase is the enzyme that helps convert testosterone into dihydrotestosterone (DHT), which is critical to normal male development. While a 5-alpha-reductase pseudohermaphrodite does have testes and Wolffian ducts, the external genitals are sized similarly to a normal female. Without intervention, an

EXPLORE FURTHER: *MIDDLESEX*

The narrator of Jeffrey Eugenides's Pulitzer Prize–winning novel *Middlesex* (New York: Farrar, Straus and Giroux, 2002) introduces himself from page 1 as the subject of a published medical study titled "Gender Identity in 5-Alpha-Reductase Pseudohermaphrodites" and then proceeds to enthrall readers with such a fine work of Greek American historical fiction that his intersex condition is soon forgotten in favor of superb storytelling. This intergenerational family saga, which spans continents, is ultimately the story of Cal Stephanides, who was born and raised as "Calliope" until as a teenager he was discovered to be more than female—a hermaphrodite.[10] Readers absorb Greek and American history from this fascinating tale, only to discover at the end that they have also been sensitized to Cal's hermaphroditic condition and its appearance at puberty. First published in 2002, the book quickly gained a huge readership and maintained a place on best-seller lists for about two years thereafter.

adult 5-alpha-reductase pseudohermaphrodite (also known as a person with 5-Alpha-Reductase Deficiency) will appear generally male, but with small external genitals and an absence of facial hair.[11]

HYPOSPADIAS AND EPISPADIAS

Hypospadias and epispadias are birth defects that are consequences of improper penile development while the embryo is forming. Normally the urethra runs the length of the penis, to form an opening at its tip, but sometimes the urethra fails to reach the tip of the penis. In hypospadias, the urethra forms an opening on the underside of the penis. In epispadias the urethra exits on the penis's upper side. Surgery can be performed to extend the urethra to the tip of the penis. If the original opening is very close to the base of the penis, such that sperm are not deposited far enough into the vagina, surgery may be necessary to facilitate natural reproduction (without requiring the assistance of reproductive technologies).[12]

EXPLORE FURTHER: HYPOSPADIAS AND EPISPADIAS ASSOCIATION

More information is available through the Hypospadias and Epispadias Association (HEA) in Somerset, Texas. Visit their website at www.heainfo.org.

FREQUENCY

Several more classifications of intersex conditions exist, all of them as complex and life changing as those we've already examined. The frequency of such conditions has not been well documented, which may help to explain the broad variation in statistics offered by differing sources. Based on the work of Dr. Anna Fausto-Sterling and her colleagues, ISNA reports the following numbers:[13]

classical congenital adrenal hyperplasia	one in 13,000 births
late onset adrenal hyperplasia	one in 66 people
vaginal agenesis	one in 6,000 births
ovotestes	one in 83,000 births
not XX and not XY	one in 1,666 births
androgen insensitivity syndrome	one in 13,000 births
partial androgen insensitivity syndrome	one in 130,000 births
Klinefelter (XXY)	one in 1,000 births
hypospasdias (urethral opening along the penile shaft)	one in 2,000 births
hypospasdias (urethral opening between the corona and the tip)	one in 770 births
Total number of people whose bodies differ from the standard male or female	one in 100 births
Total number of people receiving surgery to "normalize" genital appearance	one in 1,000 births

Every human body is unique. Like snowflakes, we appear generally the same from a distance. But when one stops to examine closely, every snowflake is unique and every human is different. Some of our variations are negligible, some slight, about 1 percent (see above) have bodies that differ from the standard male or female, and about 1 percent of these will undergo genital surgery. Physical variances between people are part of what make each person special, adding to our inherent individuality.

TO CUT OR NOT TO CUT?

In chapter 1, the development of the treatment protocol that grew out of Dr. John Money's initial research findings was discussed. Physicians subscribing to that school of thought advocate genital surgery in infancy to create genitals that appear consistent with the sex the infant is assigned. Some call this the concealment-centered model because concealment of

---

FETAL DEVELOPMENT WEBSITE

The Hospital for Sick Children's animated website clearly demonstrates how the body works. In an interactive step-by-step animation, the genital development section of the website explains how fetuses develop sexual anatomy. In addition to standard development, the site includes some variations on the standard. Go to www.sickkids.ca/childphysiology/cpwp/genital/genitalintro.htm to find this clear explanation. Then, amaze a science teacher by sharing the site's address.

---

the child's intersex status is emphasized. Contrary to this approach, the Intersex Society of North America advocates a patient-centered approach to treatment of intersex conditions. The table provided in appendix A provides a thorough comparison of intersexuality as viewed through the lens of each model. Prepared by Dr. Alice Dreger, a medical historian and ethicist at Michigan State University and a board member of ISNA, it compares responses to several basic questions from each of the two models of treatment—the concealment-centered model (developed as a result of Money's work) and the patient-centered model. One issue, two distinct viewpoints.

THE TIMES, THEY ARE A-CHANGING

Ten years ago I had never heard the word *intersex*, let alone understood that sexual anomalies existed and were actually fairly common. Times are changing. In the summer of 2004, articles about intersex conditions were prominently placed in some mainstream newspapers in the United States. Not buried deep within a section, intersex conditions and the people they affect hit the front pages of the sections in which they appeared, including the news section of the *Record* of northern New Jersey, the Sunday Styles section of the *New York Times*, and the Children First section of the Detroit *Free Press*. Perhaps one reason these stories are appearing is that as more and more people learn about the topic, they support ISNA's patient-centered model—and decry the secrecy, shame, and personal devastation associated with the concealment-centered model. News writers suggest other reasons for the prominent placement of these articles.

Medical writer Patricia Anstett of Detroit's *Free Press* attributes the attention to publicity surrounding *Middlesex*, which quickly became a best-selling novel after its publication in 2002, as well as to nationwide reports about David Reimer's death in May 2004. Anstett's article about a Michigan State University professor's activism on behalf of intersex children appeared on the front page of the *Free Press*'s Children First section.[14]

Staff writer Ruth Padawer of New Jersey's *Record* credits the front-page placement of her stories to the fact that "the condition is little known by the general public and the editors [believe the topic is] of high interest, particularly because of the nuanced and emotional issues associated with it."[15] Her articles described the experiences of various intersex people, some of whom were subjected to gender assignment surgery as infants. Betsy, one person profiled in the series, now in her forties, is an intersex activist. She was born with a long phallus, which doctors determined was a penis and therefore classified the child as male. When doctors later found both a uterus and ovaries, the baby's penis was renamed an enlarged clitoris and the child was designated female. Her surgery, the removal of most of the enlarged clitoris, left her unable to experience sexual pleasure. She likens herself to a survivor of child sexual abuse—abuse presented as medical treatment.

Another person, Deborah, was also born with an enlarged clitoris; it was larger than normal by one-fifth of an inch. When she reached eighteen months, doctors discovered testes and Deborah was renamed Thomas. With such a different anatomy, Thomas became an unhappy boy who did not fit in with other boys and, as a child, never used a public restroom. Although he knew he had an endocrine disorder, Thomas had not been told that most people with his syndrome were identified as female. When his breasts began to grow at age twelve, he was most distressed; a doctor recommended a double mastectomy and Thomas underwent the surgery at thirteen. However, his voice never deepened, his shoulders failed to broaden, and the hair on his cheeks stayed soft. Although he never did fit in as a boy, Thomas was not offered a chance to be a girl. As an adult, Thomas resumed life as Deborah and had breast reconstruction surgery. When Deborah's physical masculinity reappeared in the form of testicular cancer, she let her colleagues assume that she had "female trouble."

Another story in Padawer's article described a woman who found out she had the chromosomes of a male when she went to get her premarital blood test! Her female-appearing body lacked a cervix and uterus, but it was clear to both her and her fiancé that she was most definitely female. She is happily married now, and the couple has an adopted son, but the boy's parents have never told him about his mother's condition.

Looking again at the delivery room question "Is it a boy or a girl?" one sees that while the question is usually simple, it may have a more complex, ambiguous answer.

NOTES

1. Cheryl Chase, "What Is the Agenda of the Intersex Patient Advocacy Movement?" *Endocrinologist* 13, no. 3 (May–June 2003): 240–42; also available at www.isna.org/drupal/agenda.

2. Johns Hopkins Medicine Office of Communications and Public Affairs, "Hopkins Research Shows That Nature, Not Nurture, Determines Gender," press release, 12 May 2000, www.hopkinsmedicine.org/press/2000/may/000512.htm.

3. Claudia Kolker, "The Cutting Edge: Why Some Doctors Are Moving Away from Performing Surgery on Babies of Indeterminate Gender," *Slate*, 8 June 2004, http://slate.com/id/2102006.

4. American Educational Gender Information Service, "Intersexuality: Info and Bibliography," 1999, www.gender.org/aegis/other/article_listings/intersexuality.html.

5. "How Is Sex Determined?" *NOVA Online*, www.pbs.org/wgbh/nova/gender/determined.html.

6. This section draws heavily upon Klinefelter Syndrome & Associates, "Sex Chromosome Variations: About 47XXY," n.d., http://genetic.org/ks/scvs/47xxy.htm.

7. This section draws from Turner Syndrome Society of the United States, "Resources and Research," n.d., http://www.turner-syndrome-us.org/resource/faq.html.

8. Nelson Soucasaux, M.D., "Mayer-Rokitansky-Kuster-Hauser Syndrome (Congenital Total or Partial Absence of Uterus and Vagina)," 2002, www.mum.org/mayersyn.htm.

9. This section draws from ISNA, "Progestin Induced Virilization," 2004, www.isna.org/faq/conditions/progestin.

10. The Androgen Insensitivity Syndrome Support Group takes issue with Eugenides's use of terminology, preferring the modern term *intersex* over the outdated term *hermaphrodite* that is used in the book; see "What Is AIS?" www.medhelp.org/www/ais/21_overview.htm.

11. Carl Gold, "The Intersex Spectrum," *NOVA Online*, 2001, www.pbs.org/wgbh/nova/gender/spectrum.html.

12. This section draws from "What Are Hypospadias & Epispadias?" in the Frequently Asked Questions of the Hypospadias and Epispadias Association (HEA) website, www.heainfo.org/shell_resources.htm.

13. Intersex Society of North America, "Frequency: How Common Are Intersex Conditions?" www.isna.org/faq/frequency.html.

14. Patricia Anstett, "A Different Kind of Normal: MSU Professor Leads a Change for Children with Physical Abnormalities," *Free Press* (Detroit), 10 July 2004.

15. Ruth Padawer, e-mail message to the author, 6 June 2005. Her articles "Intersexuals Struggle to Find Their Identity" and "A 10-Year-Old's Decision: 'Will I be Kelli or Max?'" appeared in the *Record* (New Jersey) on 25 and 26 July 2004.

5

Brain Sex: Is It All in Your Head?

HELPING PEOPLE UNDER-
STAND GENDER ISSUES
HELPS YOU, TOO

SCIENCE OF BRAIN SEX

Consider the number of times you've explained something away because of a person's gender. Wouldn't it be nice to think that males and females behave the way they do because of the ways their brains are wired and that the common strengths and failings of both genders are inevitable and/or inescapable? If science were to prove that "men are from Mars and women are from Venus,"[1] we could stop trying so hard to get members of the opposite sex to understand our point of view.

The best-seller *Brain Sex: The Real Difference between Men and Women*, cowritten by geneticist Anne Moir, Ph.D., and journalist David Jessel (New York: Dell Publishing, 1992), builds a strong argument behind this theory. The work remains controversial because the scientific community has yet to decisively settle the matter. The authors of *Brain Sex* argue that the brain's sex is determined *in utero*. Simply put, they contend that exposure to testosterone over a period of time during the first trimester of pregnancy causes a female brain to become male.

Although Moir and Jessel want readers to believe that brain sex is wholly developed by birth, other researchers have since documented further brain sex differentiation in humans between two and four years of age. Furthermore, in late 2003, research led by Dr. Eric Vilain, an assistant professor of human genetics and urology at the University of California at Los Angeles, identified fifty-four genes that play a role in the

Figure 5.1. A look inside Garret's head

expression of sex in a fetus before hormones are ever released.[2] Whether brain sex—the functional structure of the brain along gender lines—is determined in the womb or at a later stage is still a matter for debate among scientists, as is the theory that male and female brains do, in fact, differ structurally along gender lines.

Researchers in Amsterdam doing postmortem brain studies have determined that the hypothalamus influences sexual behavior. In the male and female brains, the hypothalamus develops differently, and in transsexual brains the hypothalamus more closely resembles that of the opposite sex from which it was born.[3] As tempting as it is to believe that male and female brains are structurally different, the matter of greater importance to readers is that the gender with which one identifies (gender identity), and the sex(es) to which one is physically attracted (sexual identity), seem also to be seated in the mind.

In this arena, too, scientists hold differing opinions. In addition to the simple male/female dichotomy to which most of society adheres, some multidimensional theories of gender exist. One psychotherapist, Carl W. Bushong, Ph.D., posits a theory of gender consisting of five attributes. Two of these—genetic inheritance and physical appearance—were addressed in chapter 4. The other three are all based in the brain or mind. One is brain sex, or the actual physical structure of the brain, as mentioned above. Another is sexual orientation, or the sex of the persons to whom one feels sexually drawn—those persons who arouse one's love or sexual interest.

While some people believe that one's sexuality—be it homosexuality, bisexuality, or heterosexuality—is a choice, others disagree. In 1991, after conducting postmortem research on the brains of gay men who had died of AIDS, Simon LeVay published a paper in the American journal *Science* noting that the structure of the hypothalamus in homosexuals differs from that in heterosexuals. LeVay's research findings were among those that led to the popular media discussion of the possibility of a "gay gene."[4]

The third brain-based attribute in Bushong's theory of gender is that of gender identity—which gender a person perceives his or her sex to be. Bushong also called this our subjective gender or our "sexual self-map." What prompts our self-perceptions of gender is not wholly understood, possibly because it is the least researched of the attributes, but "like pain, [gender identity] is unambiguously felt but one is unable to prove or display it to others."[6] When one's gender identity does not match his or her biological sex, a state of such unease results that the condition is currently known as "gender dysphoria." This condition, whose prevalence is believed to affect up to 3 percent of the human population, is a natural variance, like the minority whose sexual orientation is homosexual. Indeed, Vilain's 2003 UCLA study may help explain transgenderism.[7] Continued scientific research is needed before any clear answers may be realized.

If you've ever heard that gender variance occurs only within the human population and that sex and gender roles in nature are either male or female and always heterosexual, you've been misinformed. For purposes of reproduction, some plants rely on cross-pollination but others self-pollinate and reproduce by themselves. In the ocean, the male seahorse is the one who carries the eggs, bears the young, and then raises them. On land, earthworms are both male and female, and some snails reproduce by mating with themselves. Homosexuality, too, is evident in the animal kingdom. Zoologists have documented homosexual behavior among birds, bats, sheep, and dolphins, to name just a few.[8]

FACTS OF NATURE

A clue that hormones may not be the complete key to gender roles is evident in the hyena population. Female hyenas have more testosterone than male hyenas. Indeed, the clitoris of the female hyena looks much like a long penis. Sexually, the female hyena mounts the male from the rear. What do these facts do to our assumptions that the male of a species is the one who has more testosterone, and the male who initiates the sexual coupling?[5]

...EVERYONE'S HEAD IS UNIQUE

Figure 5.2.   What's on Grant's mind?

ONE CHILD'S BEGINNING

The accompanying photographs document the growth of a child who was given the gender assignment of "girl" at birth and was raised as a girl, but is clearly working on a more masculine presentation. Kael Parker was born into a female body, but his gender identity is male. (Later photos of Kael appear in chapter 7.)

Figure 5.3.   Kael, age 2, with pacifier

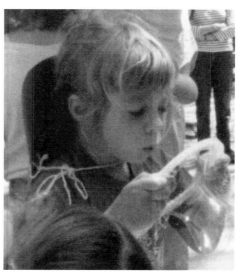

Figure 5.4.   Young Kael blowing bubbles

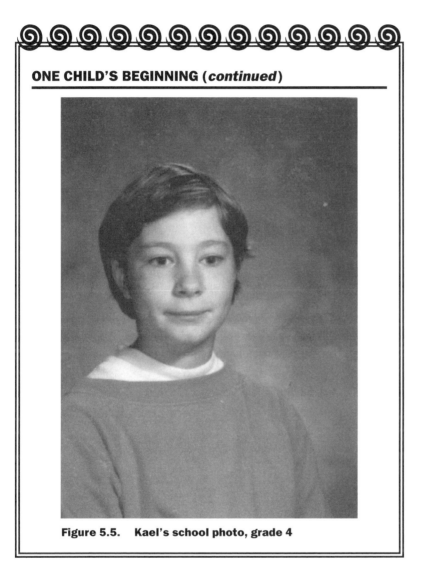

ONE CHILD'S BEGINNING (*continued*)

Figure 5.5.   Kael's school photo, grade 4

GENDER DYSPHORIA

Not so long ago, homosexuality was considered a mental illness by the medical establishment. It was seen as a treatable deviation from the norm. Homosexuality was thought to be a curable illness, and many went to great lengths to either cure themselves or to get help for a family member or friend. In 1973, the Board of Directors of the American Psychiatric Association (APA) determined that homosexuality as a diagnosis was to be removed from the APA's Diagnostic and Statistical Manual (DSM) of illnesses. But the next manual published, the *DSM-III* in 1980, included "ego dystonic homosexuality," a diagnosis for those *distressed* about their homosexual feelings. After much debate, this diagnosis was also removed, and the 1987 revised edition of the *DSM-III* held only the slightest trace of it through the diagnosis of "sexual disorders not otherwise specified," which could be used when a patient experienced continued distress about unremitting homosexual attractions. Beyond the confines of the United States, the World Health Organization (WHO) continued to include homosexuality as a diagnosis in its *International Classification of Diseases* manual, 9th edition (*ICD-9*); however, in the 1992 publication of the *ICD-10*, WHO also dropped homosexuality as a medical disease or disorder.[9]

Today, the APA's *DSM-IV* includes "Gender Identity Disorder" as a psychiatric diagnosis. This diagnosis allows professionals to label the circumstance of feeling at odds with the gender assigned to a person by society. Having this diagnosis may help one gain access to medical treatment (such as hormone therapy or surgery), but it also labels the person as having a mental illness. The diagnosis applies to persons who are gender dysphoric, whose sense of gender identity and of anatomical sex do not match and who find the incongruity anxiety-provoking. Struggling to identify one's own gender is emotionally draining.

INCLUSIVE SITE

Visitors to the International Foundation for Gender Education website (www.ifge.org) are welcomed with an optimistic statement about gender identity: "We promote the understanding and acceptance of *All People*: Transgender, Transsexual, Crossdresser, Agender, Gender Queer, Intersex, Two Spirit, Drag King, Drag Queen, Queer, Straight, Butch, Femme, Homosexual, Bisexual, Heterosexual, and of course—You!"

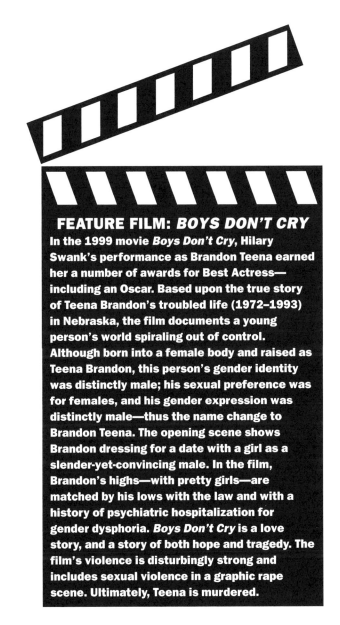

FEATURE FILM: *BOYS DON'T CRY*

In the 1999 movie *Boys Don't Cry*, Hilary Swank's performance as Brandon Teena earned her a number of awards for Best Actress— including an Oscar. Based upon the true story of Teena Brandon's troubled life (1972–1993) in Nebraska, the film documents a young person's world spiraling out of control. Although born into a female body and raised as Teena Brandon, this person's gender identity was distinctly male; his sexual preference was for females, and his gender expression was distinctly male—thus the name change to Brandon Teena. The opening scene shows Brandon dressing for a date with a girl as a slender-yet-convincing male. In the film, Brandon's highs—with pretty girls—are matched by his lows with the law and with a history of psychiatric hospitalization for gender dysphoria. *Boys Don't Cry* is a love story, and a story of both hope and tragedy. The film's violence is disturbingly strong and includes sexual violence in a graphic rape scene. Ultimately, Teena is murdered.

CHALLENGING GENDER IN SCHOOLS

According to an article by Tracy Jan in the *Boston Globe*, a transition has been going smoothly for a nine-year-old resident of a town north of Boston.[10] Born female, the child began identifying as male at age two. The parents report that as a toddler, the child would rip dresses off of her body. In

2005, at age nine, the child returned to school after a winter vacation requesting to be treated as a boy. The change was smoothly incorporated into the public elementary school, and the child previously known as Mary is now addressed as Marc.[11] Marc's classmates are young enough to have taken the change in stride—being more concerned with the lunch menu than with a classmate's name—and their parents have been good about the change as well. Those parents who did call the school with questions were most often concerned about which bathroom Marc now uses and responded positively upon hearing that he uses a separate facility altogether. Not every gender-dysphoric child has had such positive support from his/her school system.

Jan's article also cites the case of a fifteen-year-old student in the Brockton, Massachusetts, public schools who was born with male anatomy but who identified as female. In 1999, the student was prohibited from wearing feminine attire to school and the case was taken into the courts. The following year, a Massachusetts Superior Court ruling allowed the transgender male student to wear female clothing in school.

An article by Julia Reischel in the *Broward-Palm Beach New Times* tells the story of a five-year-old Floridian born with male anatomy who claims to be female.[12] The child is set to enter kindergarten in fall 2006, where she will be called by a feminine version of her name and referred to with female pronouns. She will be free to dress as she likes within uniform restrictions. Her teacher will work with her family to make her happy, and very likely most students and some teachers will be unaware of her anatomical sex.[13]

SELF-PERCEPTION

A person's gender identity is an integral part of the self. When it conflicts with the physical sex of the body and with the messages the person receives about society's expectations for the individual's gender expression, it can leave a person feeling extremely isolated. One FTM transgender teen expresses this in his poem "Home is Where . . . ," written when he was nineteen

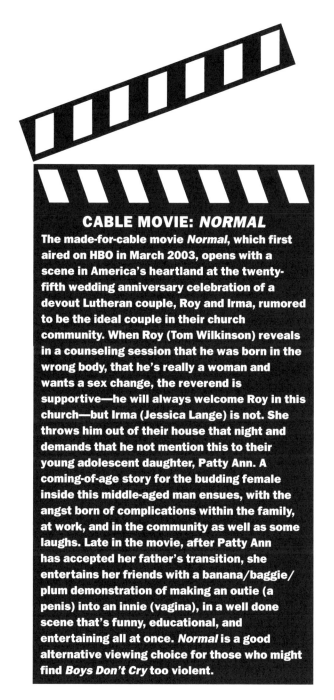

CABLE MOVIE: *NORMAL*
The made-for-cable movie *Normal*, which first aired on HBO in March 2003, opens with a scene in America's heartland at the twenty-fifth wedding anniversary celebration of a devout Lutheran couple, Roy and Irma, rumored to be the ideal couple in their church community. When Roy (Tom Wilkinson) reveals in a counseling session that he was born in the wrong body, that he's really a woman and wants a sex change, the reverend is supportive—he will always welcome Roy in this church—but Irma (Jessica Lange) is not. She throws him out of their house that night and demands that he not mention this to their young adolescent daughter, Patty Ann. A coming-of-age story for the budding female inside this middle-aged man ensues, with the angst born of complications within the family, at work, and in the community as well as some laughs. Late in the movie, after Patty Ann has accepted her father's transition, she entertains her friends with a banana/baggie/plum demonstration of making an outie (a penis) into an innie (vagina), in a well done scene that's funny, educational, and entertaining all at once. *Normal* is a good alternative viewing choice for those who might find *Boys Don't Cry* too violent.

years old. The accompanying photos were taken during the poet's childhood and adolescence.

The people who contributed their personal narratives to this volume all spoke of an enormous sense of isolation as they

PERSONAL REFLECTION: "HOME IS WHERE . . ."
BY DJT, TRANNY BOY, AGE 19

I have lived in seedy trailers,
in fancy homes with art like museums,
in cars with no destination,
in hippie paradises with artists and goats,
in cookie-cutter suburbs,
and apartments where everyone spoke Spanish in the halls.

I have lived in places that felt like home
and places that tried to convince me they were homes,
when in truth they held nothing of me—
of who I am and what makes me feel real.

So who am I?

Am I the girl in the skirt on Easter,
smiling for the camera,
crossing my legs in church?

Am I the kid in the rag-tag denim
with the dirt-stained hands and the mischievous grin,
dreaming and scheming, avoiding the law?

Am I the one with the slicked-down hair,
the one they call "Sir"
with a powerful handshake and believable lies?

Which one is me?

Today—today I am none of these,
But yesterday, and on other yesterdays,
I have been them all and a hundred more—
A hundred who had different ideas of home
And faces I would no longer recognize . . .

PERSONAL REFLECTION (*continued*)

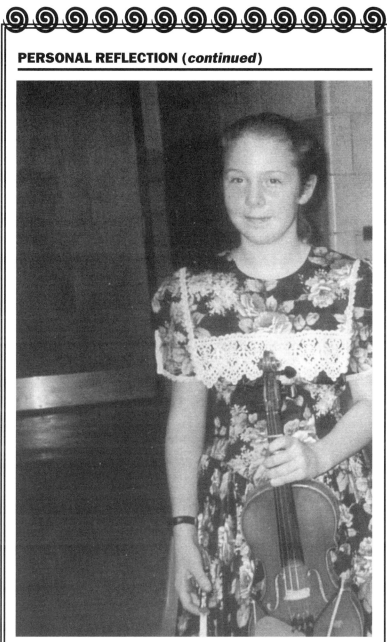

Figure 5.6.   The poem's author poses at her violin recital, age 10 or 11.

(*continued*)

PERSONAL REFLECTION (*continued*)

Figure 5.7.
Here she is before
a dance, age 14.

PERSONAL REFLECTION (*continued*)

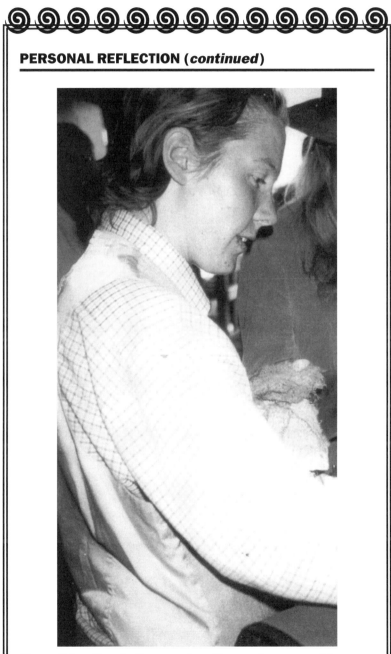

Figure 5.8.   Here is the poem's author again, now an 18-year-old male, cleaning up after a Silverton Gun Fighters' show.

sought to have their incongruent gender identities, roles or expectations, and expressions meet comfortably. Our self-perceptions of sexual identity and orientation are such integral parts of who we are that many spend a lifetime seeking acceptance in society—simply for being ourselves.

Indeed, the years of adolescence and early adulthood are a time of self-discovery and self-definition, a time when people often decide who they are (and what they stand for) and seek to accept themselves. Unfortunately, in the process of self-definition, we often resort to the overly simplistic labels readily available—for biological sex: male, female, intersex; for sexual orientation: straight, gay, lesbian, bisexual; for gender identity: male, female, transgender; for political affiliation or leanings: Democrat, Republican, left, right, center; for religion: Christian, Muslim, Hindu, Jew; and so on. The catch is that by using these labels we mislead ourselves (and others) through vastly oversimplifying who we are. Acceptance, of oneself or of another, based on such arbitrary labels unjustly pigeonholes the labeled person into a box that just might not fit and gives the observer a distorted, stilted view of the labeled person's identity or beliefs. In addition, such labels provide roles that we may allow to limit us. Finally, if our upbringing taught us that being X, Y, or Z is undesirable—even bad—how are we to accept and love ourselves when we wear that label?

MALCOLM'S STORY

A ninety-minute documentary film appeared in 2005 respectfully recording the story of one young man's journey from gender confusion to self-acceptance. Produced by Filmworks, Inc., in conjunction with the United Church of Christ (UCC), *Call Me Malcolm* is about a twenty-seven-year-old UCC seminary student who was born Miriam and perceived by others to be a girl but who always felt like a brother to his two siblings. Confused by a society that insisted he be someone other than he knew himself to be, Malcolm entered the seminary seeking answers and "hoping to reconcile the conflict between his heart and the things he was being taught in his home church." He first heard the word *transgender* around that time and the idea resonated with his own experience.

In *Call Me Malcolm*, producers Joseph Parlagreco and Kierra Chase document his journey with care, beginning as he enters his final year at seminary and traveling with him on a road trip across the United States, where he calls on a variety of people who share their views of gender, faith, and love with him. On the way, he finds acceptance and gains understanding that will help to shape his life path.[14]

UNCONDITIONAL LOVE

When a person's sexual anatomy is at odds with his or her gender identity, the brain is likely to win out. Recently, Peter, an anatomical boy, age five, stated unequivocally "I'm a girl" to his little sister Emily.[15] Is this a passing phase? An afternoon of make-believe? Or is it the statement of a deeply rooted sense of self?

I know Peter; he is a gentle child. His behaviors at play have long had his mother expecting that her son could grow up to be effeminate or gay. The boisterous nature of Emily's rough-and-tumble play serves to make Peter's absence of boy behaviors more noticeable in their home. Peter's mother has always said that she is ready to love him however he may grow up, and she recognizes that her son may face discomfort, even pain, if his eventual choice does not match society's expectations for him. When she told me about his recent declaration, she acknowledged that he may have even greater hurdles in his future than she had envisioned might be possible.

Some of the young people who contributed to this book assert that they knew their gender clearly before entering elementary school and were confused by the adults who insisted the child's gender must align with his or her anatomical sex. My friend, Peter and Emily's mother, is aware that gender identity may be firmly in place in a child's early years. Even so, she is not ready to draw any conclusions so soon. For now, she will continue listening to her children and watching their behavior;

maintaining an open, loving home for them; and using care to avoid pressuring either Peter or Emily into stereotypical gender roles. Her children are lucky to be raised with such unconditional love, but isn't that all any of us want? To be accepted and loved for who we are?

NOTES

1. *Men Are from Mars, Women Are from Venus* (1992) was the first in a series of similarly titled self-help books about relationships written by psychologist and author John Gray, Ph.D.

2. Judy Foreman, "The Biological Basis of Homosexuality," *Boston Globe*, Health/Science section, 2 December 2003.

3. "Transgender Teens," Discovery Health Channel, 2003.

4. Lesley Rogers, *Sexing the Brain* (New York: Columbia University Press, 2001).

5. Kate Bornstein, *Gender Outlaw: On Men, Women, and the Rest of Us* (New York: Routledge, 1994), 56.

6. Carl W. Bushong, "The Multi-Dimensionality of Gender," www.transgendercare.com/guidance/multi.htm.

7. Foreman, "Biological Basis of Homosexuality."

8. James Owen, "Homosexual Activity among Animals Stirs Debate," *National Geographic News*, 23 July 2004, http://news.nationalgeographic.com/news/2004/07/0722_040722_gayanimal.html.

9. Gregory M. Herek, "Facts about Homosexuality and Mental Health," 2006, http://psychology.ucdavis.edu/rainbow/html/facts_mental_health.html.

10. Tracy Jan, "Methuen School Faces Parents' Queries on Student's Gender Issue," *Boston Globe*, 5 March 2005.

11. Mary and Marc are pseudonyms used in Jan's article. The child's parents have successfully kept his identity shielded from public scrutiny. The only identifying information to the public has been that the child requested a simple name change—changing the feminine name given at birth ever-so-slightly to make it a masculine name.

12. Julia Reischel, "See Dick Be Jane," *Broward-Palm Beach New Times*, 18 May 2006, www.newtimesbpb.com/Issues/2006-05-18/news/feature.html.

13. Julia Reischel, e-mail message to the author, 3 July 2006.

14. As of this writing, *Call Me Malcolm* has yet to be released on DVD for home viewing, but clips can be viewed and a screening found or arranged through the film's website at http://callmemalcolm.com.

15. Peter and Emily's names have been changed to protect their identity and that of their family.

6 Introduction to Gender Conversations

EXPLORING GENDER

Exploring gender with a group—whether in a youth group, a classroom, or a gay–straight alliance (GSA)—can be an enlightening experience. Becoming aware of our own deeply held gender expectations and beliefs is often surprising, especially to those of us who like to think of ourselves as open-minded and accepting. In this chapter, you'll find a few exercises to help unearth those preconceptions you harbor, as well as some activities, films, and readings focused on gender roles and gender-based language. Try some out in a group of people with whom you feel safe, and you may broaden your own horizons.

ADVERTISING IMAGERY

The members of your GSA, class, or youth group may not be sure where to begin a discussion about gender. Images encountered frequently in daily life may provide a place to start. Look around. What messages about gender are implicit in the images encountered?

Savvy consumers know that advertising is designed to encourage us to purchase a product or service, but how often do we look beneath the surface of the ads? Here's an exercise to try with a group.

Have each participant bring in several full-page advertisements featuring people as models. Or, bring an assortment of magazines to the group and spend a few minutes together flipping through them. Tear out advertisements that catch your eye without regard to why you think they snagged your attention. Next, line the walls with the print advertisements. (Use masking tape or sticky tack with care. You'll want to leave the walls looking as good as they did before you started.) Stand back. Consider the images in silence for a couple of minutes, then regroup for the discussion phase.

Together, go around the group once to elicit people's initial reactions to the collection or to specific individual images. Allot each speaker a limited time, perhaps one minute, then move on promptly to the next person. What do the images and words say to the viewers about gender or gender roles? What unstated "promises" do the ads appear to be making? What gender-based messages are the images conveying? How many of them use sex as a selling tool? Which ones are blatant, and which are subtle? How? What else do you find remarkable about the images?

After working your way through this list of questions, and any your group has chosen to add, what general conclusions can your group draw—both about advertising and about gender in advertising—based on this exercise? Lastly, allot a minute to each speaker to report on his or her experience with this exercise. What surprised the participants? What did the participants learn from the exercise?

BEFORE AND AFTER

Before proceeding to the films below, have group members consider figure 6.1, the cartoon where Grant is having trouble deciding what to wear. Elicit brief written responses: What thoughts come to mind? Ask group members to jot their ideas on a sheet of paper to be reconsidered at the end of this chapter.

THERE'S NO PLACE LIKE HOME

Pull up a chair to watch a video. First have a group member borrow a copy of *That's a Family*. (Try public and school libraries before video stores.) Although the film is geared for

Figure 6.1.   Grant has trouble choosing an outfit.

younger audiences (ages kindergarten through eighth grade), it is also used with adult groups. The images it provides can be good conversation starters. *That's a Family*, a thirty-five-minute educational film by Women's Educational Media released in 2000, has children speaking about their family experiences. The face of the American family has changed since *Ozzie and Harriet* and *Leave It to Beaver*; this film emphasizes the diversity of those changes.

After viewing the film, discuss what you've seen. What did people find surprising, informative, or thought-provoking? How do the families in the documentary compare to participants' family experiences? What can be said about gender roles after viewing the film? Is this a film you would want to share with younger children (siblings, relatives, or a student group)? Why or why not?

A second film to consider is *Ma Vie En Rose* (My Life in Pink), a ninety-minute feature film about the a little boy who feels he's a girl. Directed by Alan Berliner, this 1997 film is rated R. Although the soundtrack is in French, the film has English subtitles. *Ma Vie En Rose* deftly captures one child's struggle for acceptance in a world rife with gender role expectations that don't fit his personal identity. After borrowing a copy of the film from a local library, pop the popcorn and settle in. Viewers will want to watch for the reactions of the child's family members, neighbors, and "friends" and the father's employer.

The discussion questions following this film focus around cultural and societal expectations. What are the varied reactions you see in the film? With which characters do you identify? What reasons do you attribute to each character's behavior? How does the film challenge your preconceptions of family relations, of employer–family relations, and of neighborhood expectations?

To conclude the video portion of the group's gender exploration, have a member locate and borrow a copy of the made-for-cable movie *Normal*, which we discussed in chapter 5. Written and directed by Jane Anderson, this 2003 feature-length family drama is set in America's heartland, in a conservative, rural town, and focuses on a transsexual adult. After twenty-five years of marriage, Roy tells his family and community that he wishes to become "Ruth." Watch how this community reacts, and who ultimately comes forward to support Roy's transition. His family—an adolescent daughter, adult son, and wife—his pastor and religious community, and his employer and coworkers all play significant roles in Roy's life.

Following the film, begin the group discussion by considering the same questions used for *Ma Vie En Rose*. Talk over the role of each family member and the responses of each group member. How would each of you react to such a pronouncement by your own parent or significant adult role model? What gender roles do each of your adult role models play now? How would the sex change of one of these adults impact each group member and that person's place in society? What have the three films added to your understanding of gender roles?

GENDER ROLE MEMORIES

Another exercise involves reading, writing, and sharing. First, list what you remember about gender messages you received growing up. Did your household insist that boys take out the trash, while girls worked in the kitchen? For what behaviors did you receive positive gender messages like "Thattaboy!" or "Such a little lady!" and how did such comments make you feel? Can you remember a time when you were explicitly taught to behave as a girl or a boy? How did you feel about the message? Did you welcome the instruction and eagerly seek to please your instructor, or did you chafe against being forced to behave like one gender or the other?

Next, ask yourself what you expect of a boy? A girl? Read Cal Burnap's "The Excavation" aloud together. Discuss the concept of an adult who was at one time female choosing to identify as male, and as a "boy" rather than as a "man." Consider why this choice is preferable for Cal. Imagine yourself in the future; what is your body like? Can you imagine yourself in the future, but without a body? Or, with a body of the opposite sex? Try it. What did you find out? Imagine your best friend or a close sibling going through the struggle for self that Cal has. How would you react? Consider both how you would like to imagine yourself reacting and how you think you would really react.

Cal's experience allows us to better understand some of the complexities of living across gender lines. Every personal narrative provides a bit of insight into a world beyond our own realm of experience. If you find such understanding gratifying, examine the Resources at the end of this book. A wealth of tales such as Cal's are available for those who are curious and willing to explore.

PERSONAL EXPERIENCE: "THE EXCAVATION" BY CALVIN MADDOX BURNAP, AGE 22, SEATTLE, WA

Attempting to put my life down in words is overwhelming. I cram constant inner dialogue onto crisp white pages—attempting to bottle up all the air in the universe. There has not been a time in my life when I have not contemplated where I stand in the world of gender. So few times have I been able to write for the eyes of others about my gender. It has been painfully clear to me, in the eyes of society, what I do not understand.

At four, I vowed never to wear another dress. At six, I bought all my shoes in the boys' department. I wanted to cut all my hair off. At eight, I could not understand why my friends wanted to trade stickers instead of playing tag. I idolized Pee Wee Herman, and Ken's flawless Barbie leg mysteriously fell off. When I was nine, someone told me Melissa Etheridge was a lesbian; they were horrified, while I was clueless. I began to fit in at ten by telling my friend that I had a crush on a boy named Brian—he was the only one who could beat me at a math game. At eleven I read *Am I Blue?* (edited by Marion Dane Bauer, 1994), an anthology of short stories by young adult authors about queer youth. I wrote on my computer, "I don't think that I am blue. But perhaps I am. Why don't people accept blue people? It makes no sense." I promptly forgot about the book and moved on.

Some days I would dress as a boy. Some days, because I thought it was important, I dressed as a girl. On the days I was a girl, I agonized over every last detail. I wore my mother's makeup and let my hair down. At thirteen, I played on the boys' basketball team. At fourteen, in high school, I forgot about being a boy; I was a girl for the first four months there. By the time I was fifteen, with a haircut and a rainbow on my backpack, I had come out as a lesbian, dedicating my life to stomping through the streets, making sure people knew what I was. But, for all the books I read, I could not find myself in the word "lesbian." Lesbian meant embracing myself as a woman who loved women. I did not embrace myself as a woman; I was simply attracted to women. However, at the time I was too concerned with defining myself as gay to notice that gender issues had slipped to the back of my mind, waiting patiently to pounce on my secured identity.

By the age of nineteen I let go of issues around my sexuality. To whom I am attracted has become less and less

PERSONAL EXPERIENCE: "THE EXCAVATION" BY CALVIN MADDOX BURNAP, AGE 22, SEATTLE, WA (*continued*)

important. My friends poke fun because half my books are about queer issues, but the subjects have changed. They now focus on finding a place between and within society's two acceptable gender roles.

I see myself floating in my own private country. I occupy a land of neutrality in a world of gendered roles. Knowing what men represent in society, I do not see myself as a man. Being female, I cannot embrace society's forced guidelines for women. If I could, I would just be a boy. A sissy boy, but a boy nonetheless. A boy who never goes through puberty, that is the boy I want to be. Left to my own devices I have no gender. Unfortunately, I must inevitably leave my delusions of neutrality and enter "the real world." Choosing which bathroom to use, for example, is not my personal decision. I have to work with what society and my choices have given me. I cannot simply use the women's room because there I am vilified for my appearance. The men's room, on the other hand, poses a threat to my safety because I am not the conventional image of man. In this world I must formulate my gender. Within the context of the theory that gender is relative, I must define my gender, even if it comes down to which bathroom I am safer using.

I am not what society expects a woman to be. I am, by no means, what society expects of a man, nor do I want to be. In order to function in this society, I must find my gender relative to what I am not. Since I do not see myself as a man or a woman, I am reclaiming "boy" for myself. It embodies my lack of femininity without being overly gendered.

Often others assume that my gender of choice automatically qualifies me to pass in society as male. I choose the label *transgendered*, meaning exactly what the word implies: to transcend gender. I have little interest in becoming the polar-opposite male, because it would simply further reinforce socialized gender roles. Undergoing a physical transition is my way of actualizing the way I see myself when I have my eyes closed. I want to see my self-image reflected in the eyes of others. Being a boy is my compromise with society. Transitioning is my way of promising myself a future.

(continued)

PERSONAL EXPERIENCE: "THE EXCAVATION" BY CALVIN MADDOX BURNAP, AGE 22, SEATTLE, WA (*continued*)

Prior to deciding to transition physically through hormones and surgery, I had a very difficult time seeing myself. I could not imagine myself growing up, choosing a career, living a life, when I could not even imagine my body being part of the process. I believe that transitioning will allow me to appreciate better my femininity that has always existed. I am becoming a more whole person by creating the freedom to be a feminine, female, boy. One's life is a transition from one place to another; mine is no different. There will be a point that my physical transition from girl to boy will be complete. The measurement of such, however, is not about success living as a male. On the contrary, it is not so much that I am changing my gender but that I am re-molding my skin to fit better around the person that I am. I am excavating the boy that I am on the inside.

POWERFUL WORDS

If your group is serious about its exploration of gender issues, you may want to seek out a resource designed for classroom use and available through Tolerance.org. *The Power of Words: Examining the Language of Ethnic, Gender, and Sexual Orientation Bias* provides ten detailed lessons to help guide your explorations.[1] Beware: the strong language addressed is not for the faint of heart. Even if your group tackles only the lessons on male-bashing and gender (lesson 1), reclaiming pejorative words (lesson 4), and normative sexuality (lesson 9), you will have given yourselves much food for thought.

Other, less time-consuming activities can be found in the Spring 2005 issue of *Teaching Tolerance* magazine. This publication—which is provided free for teachers—can be obtained from the Southern Poverty Law Center in Montgomery, Alabama, or located through the Tolerance.org website by following the "For Teachers" link. The Spring 2005 issue includes "Caroline Is a Boy" by Dana Williams, an article by a teacher reflecting on a former student whose needs the high school failed to meet, as well as resource listings and classroom activities for younger students around the concept of gender.

GENDER ROLES

Next, read Julie Anne Peters's young-adult novel *Luna* alone or with a group. If you're working alone, keep a journal and imagine yourself in Regan's place. If you're working with a group, hold frequent discussions (perhaps after every few chapters). How do other views differ from your own? Does hearing others' thoughts change the way you think about the issue? What if Regan's family were your family or the family next door to you? After reading *Luna*, do you feel any different about persons choosing a gender expression other than that of the gender assigned to them at birth?

PERSONAL PHOTOGRAPHS

Have the group consider the photo spreads in this book. Figures 5.3–5.5 depict the same person, Kael Parker, when he was considered a girl. Notice how Kael had begun to present himself with a more masculine appearance as early as his fourth-grade school photo. Now turn to figures 7.2 and 7.4 in chapter 7. These depict Kael first as an older child, then as a young adult after beginning to transition from female to male. What do group members think about this collection of photos? Is there

---

CONTEMPORARY LITERATURE

Julie Anne Peters's young-adult novel *Luna* (New York: Little, Brown, 2004) is told by Regan, the younger sister of Liam—a boy who says he's a girl. Sleep-deprived from supporting her brother's late-night excursions into the role of Luna, Regan struggles with her high school studies, her home life, and her social life. As Liam slowly transitions into life as Luna, Regan watches—but with whom can she talk about it? Borrow a copy from your local library, or buy your own, because *Luna* is definitely a book not to be missed.

any question about the gender of the young man in figure 7.4? Do the presence of sideburns help viewers reach their answers to this question?

APPEARANCES CAN BE DECEIVING

Check out the A&E Television Network's 2002 documentary *Role Reversal*. Available in both DVD and VHS formats, this 100-minute broadcast can be obtained online through the AETV.com store. This feature-length reality-TV documentary raises questions about gender most people would never think to ask. Four adults, two male and two female, live together for one month in New York City, during which time they attempt to live as the opposite sex. Using therapists, coaches, counselors, stylists, and beauticians, the four switch gender roles by learning to assume the appearance, movement, voice, and attitude of their counterparts. The transformations are amazing to behold and provide profound life experiences for the four courageous adults. While the goal is temporary, the transformations are successful as each subject passes undetected in both work and social settings. Their experiences provide a bounty of material for discussion and reflection.

Recommended questions for your discussion include: What makes a man a man and a woman a woman? What role does appearance play in our lives—both as we perceive others and as others perceive us? How does this impact gender expectations? Are women necessarily vulnerable and men strong? Consider the *Role Reversal* participants' expectations and experiences. What happened when one of the men masquerading as a woman was revealed as a male in public? How do you think that revelation impacted the men who had been conversing with this "woman"? Why? Compare the participants' expectations prior to their experience with what they said afterward. How do you think the experience changed each of them? Why do you think one person dropped out just before the exit interview? How do you suppose this experience will impact that person's life in the future? And, finally, if you had all the time in the world, would you consider participating in such an experiment? Why or why not? What would you expect to gain and lose from the experience?

HOW MANY TRANSGENDER PEOPLE ARE THERE?

Now that your group has considered the concept of gender and some of the various aspects of transgender life, consider the numbers. What proportion of society is transgender? While studies have produced widely varying numbers over the years, no one has a good answer to the question, but all agree the number is exceedingly small.

Dr. Mary Ann Horton, a researcher who consults with companies, groups, and others about gender issues in the workplace, developed the image in figure 6.2 to illustrate the prevalence of transgender people in our society.[2] Her ice cream cone chart compares the vast percentage of persons who are not transgender (illustrated by the cone's wide mouth) with the small percentage of transgender individuals. Using the narrowing design of the cone to illustrate different levels of gender-crossing behaviors, she indicates how small the number of postoperative transsexuals is in comparison with the rest of

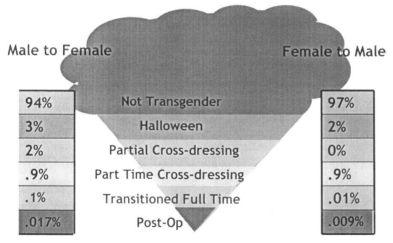

How Many Transgender People are There?

Male to Female		Female to Male
94%	Not Transgender	97%
3%	Halloween	2%
2%	Partial Cross-dressing	0%
.9%	Part Time Cross-dressing	.9%
.1%	Transitioned Full Time	.01%
.017%	Post-Op	.009%

Figure 6.2.   How many transgendered people are there? *(Mary Ann Horton, Ph.D., Red Ace Consulting Services)*

the population. The levels indicate how far people have taken their desire for transgender expression. (While the numbers for the Not Transgender, Transitioned Full-Time, and Postoperative groups are accurate, the Halloween, Partial Cross-dressing, and Part-Time Cross-dressing numbers are estimates.)[3]

The largest group of transgender people cross-dress only on rare occasions, such as Halloween. The next group cross-dresses fairly regularly but with few garments at a time, such as women who wear neckties in lieu of scarves, or men who wear ladies' undergarments beneath their everyday attire. Individuals who cross-dress completely but do so only part-time comprise the next group. Then, approaching the base of the cone, comes the group of persons who have crossed full-time into transgender life; this group consists of less than one-tenth of 1 percent of the general population. Finally, the very tip of the cone represents the tiny number of postoperative transsexuals in society. The ice cream cone illustration visually represents the transgender population in relation to the general population.

Share figure 6.2 with the group. What do members of the group think of this visual representation? Questions for discussion could include: Why do members think the numbers decrease so sharply? How many in the group have crossed gender lines for Halloween or another event involving costumes? Did they identify as transgender at the time? Do they now? Who in the group would now consider cross-dressing for Halloween, and how have the group discussions impacted that decision? What might it feel like to live as a person at any of these levels?

IT'S A WRAP

Now that you and your group have had these conversations about gender, ask yourselves how the photos, readings, films, and discussions have changed your perceptions of gender. In what ways will you now look at the world around you differently than you did before this experience? In what ways do you think it will change your interactions with very young children, with androgynous persons, or with people whose

CONTEMPORARY LITERATURE

Do you enjoy stand-up comics' monologues? Could you ever imagine yourself in the comic's place on stage? In Sharon Dennis Wyeth's young-adult novel *Orphea Proud* (New York: Delacorte Press, 2004), Orphea turns her own story—of identity, family, and prejudice—into a dramatic performance. In so doing she proves that one's life can be tragic and still garner audience laughter. Check out her story!

gender expression somehow conflicts with your expectation of their gender role?

Revisit figure 6.1, the cartoon of Grant deciding what to wear. Now that you have examined gender so critically, how do your group members respond to the cartoon? Again, elicit brief written responses. Retrieve the written responses made before your group viewed any films. Have group members compare their current and earlier responses. Is there any difference? What differences can you see, and why do you think the differences exist?

CONTINUING THE CONVERSATION

After pursuing the suggestions in this chapter, you and your group will be equipped to consider gender more fully than before. Some of you may wish to continue the journey. On your way, do visit the Resources section at the end of this book to find other organizations, websites, books, magazines, pamphlets, and films. These provide a wealth of information and will allow your group to design its own gender conversations.

NOTES

1. The *Power of Words* curriculum, by Janet Lockhart and Susan M. Shaw, is available at www.tolerance.org/teach/web/power_of_words/index.jsp.

2. This section draws from Mary Ann Horton's report "The Cost of Transgender Health Benefits," 2006, available at www.tgender.net/taw/thbcost.html.

3. Mary Ann Horton, Ph.D., e-mail message to author, 5 September 2005.

7 Transformations

HELPING PEOPLE UNDER-
STAND GENDER ISSUES
HELPS YOU, TOO

CHOOSING TO CHANGE

At some point, the boy who feels like a girl, the homosexual who lives deeply closeted, the middle-aged man (or woman) who feels driven for a last youthful fling, the untested songwriter who is tired of simply waiting tables for a living, or any one of us may decide the time is right to make a change. Meeting the expectations of society may be comfortable in some respects, but sometimes the need to be ourselves overrides the aim to please. When the issue is a deep-seated need within a person, she or he can either continue with the status quo or make the change that feels right.

Some of these changes are more drastic than others. The middle-aged man who buys a new sports car and drives about with the top down may turn a head or two or set tongues to wagging, but for the most part the worst he will face is some ribbing from his buddies. Today, even the closeted homosexual can come out as a lesbian or a gay man in most parts of the United States without her or his world grinding to a halt. Certainly, some social discomfort is to be expected, and some families experience irreparable rifts, but as more and more people come out, gay life becomes more commonplace in the eyes of those who did not accept it previously.

For transgender persons, even though their stories have begun to work their way into prime-time television, full acceptance appears to be a long way off. Transgender characters as portrayed on television shows such as *NYPD*

Blue, *Law & Order*, and *Boston Public* were not accepted in the mainstream; indeed, in some cases, they were portrayed as victims of homicide.

Despite the risks, many people experience a driving need to reshape their life around their true self. For the transgender person, there is no one right or wrong way to make such a change. One must change to the extent that he or she feels comfortable—until feeling at home in his or her body. Some persons will be satisfied by simply dressing and acting in the manner of their chosen sex and have no desire or need to change their physical bodies through the use of hormones or surgery. Some may make temporary cosmetic wardrobe changes, much the way a girdle controls a midriff bulge, lasting only as long as the garment is worn. For others, hormones cause the body to appear more feminine or masculine. Those who choose to make surgical changes have a far greater need to inhabit a body that brings their sex in line with their gender identity; surgery is invasive, permanent, and very expensive.

WORLD'S FIRST FAMOUS TRANSSEXUAL

In 1952 Christine Jorgensen garnered worldwide attention by becoming the world's first public male-to-female transsexual. Stepping into the limelight following her surgery, Christine became a media magnet who intrigued the public for years to come. Much attention was given to her appearance, for her actions flew in the face of the notion that sex and gender were unchangeable. Jorgensen, an ex-GI, was a beautiful, charismatic, and successful woman.

Figure 7.1. How well does a mirror reflect one's self-image? Tera's mirror-image leaves her ready to scream.

Changing genders is a life-altering process. The enormity of the process the trans person undergoes is tremendous. While any outcome of transitioning is acceptable if it helps a person to feel more whole or real, the public nature of the process itself can put a trans person at risk. The seemingly simple choice of which restroom to use can become fraught with anxiety or even danger. A male transitioning to female may be hard-pressed to find an appropriate restroom until ze can successfully pass most of the time. Imagine someone who appears to be a man, wearing a dress, entering a large public restroom, and think for a minute how the other patrons might react. While a person who appears to be a woman dressed as a man—wearing pants, or a suit and tie—is more likely to be accepted in a women's restroom or able to pass in the men's room (a discussion of standing to urinate is located later in this chapter), ze still risks disdain or ridicule, at the least. But more goes into a gender transition than clothing. Not only are males and females built differently but they also tend to move (walk, sit, stand, or gesture) and speak differently. A trans person must be an excellent student, observing nuances in tone and mannerisms, then molding his or her own speech and movement to fit society's expectations of the gender role ze is presenting.

REACTIONS OF FAMILY AND COLLEAGUES

Major transitions result in permanent changes in a person's life. Coming out to one's family, whether as transgender or homosexual, a person cannot be sure of unconditional support. Many families do not survive such announcements and may sever ties. The numbers of homeless gay, lesbian, and transgender teens continue to increase in the United States as youth become increasingly bold about asserting individual identities. Some teens are subjected to violence in their homes, and they may choose to leave a bad situation or may find themselves put out on the street. As open-minded as any parents perceive themselves to be, the news that a child wishes to change his or her gender, or to love a person of the same sex, can be devastating to the parent's perception of the child and of the child's future. Even if the child is an adult living independently from the family of origin, to parents the child is still their baby. Transitioning while at school or working in an office creates its own set of challenges. Some people will doubtless be supportive and eager to understand, but others may be uncomfortable, distrustful, or

HELPING PARENTS TO UNDERSTAND

TransProud, OutProud's website for transgender youth (www.transproud.com), includes a welcome page for parents of transgender children at www.transproud.com/parents.html.

PERSONAL REFLECTION: "GROWING UP QUEER"
BY KAEL PARKER

My story is not unlike many other people's stories. I knew I was different from a very young age. When we played "Dukes of Hazzard" out in the yard, I was always Luke Duke, even when my sister wasn't around to play Daisy. Then, in second grade I remember coming home from school and my next door neighbor couldn't wait to tell me about the people he'd seen on the talk show that day, women who used to be men; he knew that as soon as I heard about it that I'd want to do it too. In that instant, I felt so amazing, until I heard my mother and his mother laughing at the idea that anyone would ever actually do something like that, and what freaks they must be. I wonder if they knew how small that made me feel or how for the next few days I felt so wrong about myself that I didn't want to leave my room to go to school or even to play outside.

I could tell you about how I heard the girls on the playground talking about why you should always sleep on your back, because it would make your breasts come in bigger and faster, and how from that time on I always made sure I fell asleep on my stomach, hoping mine would never show up. I could tell you how, when at the age of sixteen I finally got my period, I didn't rush to tell my mother the way my sister had, but instead I cried and searched the bathroom for a pad and stole tampons from my sister because I was too ashamed to buy them for myself.

But I also have stories about times when everything seemed perfect. Summers spent outside in the sun, riding bikes and trading baseball cards with the other boys down the street. Running through the sprinkler with our shirts off in my backyard. Talking about the girls we wanted to marry when we grew up, before any of us were old enough to understand that things weren't going to work out as easily as we all expected.

I remember sitting out on the front steps with my father, watching a summer thunderstorm, when he said to me that he wished I'd been born a boy because things would be so much easier for me, and how I should really start thinking about changing some things because it just wasn't right for a young lady to go around acting the way I did. I remember having to fight my church before they let me choose Saint Francis to be my patron saint for Confirmation, because I was a girl and he

(continued)

109

PERSONAL REFLECTION: "GROWING UP QUEER" BY KAEL PARKER (*continued*)

was a man and that just wasn't allowed. I remember waking up in a sweat the first time I had a dream where I had a male body, scared by how good it made me feel to see myself that way. I was twelve years old.

There was never a time when I decided that I was going to conform to what other people wanted me to be, it just kind of happened that way. Through high school I grew my hair long, wore dresses to the prom, played softball . . . it never occurred to me that I had other options. I still wasn't a *girl* girl though. I was thirteen the first time I ever heard the word *butch* used to describe me. I had no idea what it meant, but I knew it had to be bad. I wasn't like the popular girls who wore makeup and did their nails and always had a boyfriend. By no means was I one of the boys, either. The guys down the street got older, too, and made it clear that I couldn't hang out with them anymore. I wasn't allowed to look at their dirty magazines, I couldn't play on the same baseball teams. They all got girlfriends, and I was left behind.

So I coasted along on my own. I got used to being alone. Something about me was just different. I started to feel really close to some of my girl friends, wanting to spend all of my time with them, thinking about how nice it would be to be together with them all the time. Sure, in the back of my mind I had thought, "Am I gay?" but no way, that couldn't be me. I remember sitting in my bedroom, eating McDonald's with a friend while we watched an Indigo Girls video on TV, and for the first time actually letting myself feel sexually attracted to a woman. I don't know how I kept a straight face while inside I felt like everything was turning upside-down. It was almost a year later that I first told another person about what I began feeling that day.

I went to college, I got a girlfriend, and suddenly I was out to my family and friends as a lesbian. I thought I'd finally figured everything out, that this must be why I'd felt so different for all those years. For a while, things were making sense to me again. People were accepting me for who I was, or at least for the person I was showing them. But if everything was better, why did my stomach sink when my partner told me how handsome I was, or when she said she knew I would make a good daddy someday? She bought me a copy of *Stone Butch Blues* for my birthday and I read it cover-to-cover in two days. I

PERSONAL REFLECTION: "GROWING UP QUEER"
BY KAEL PARKER (*continued*)

felt like I should be taking notes, somehow documenting what I was feeling as I read. For the first time in my life, I found my feelings and experience echoed back to me in someone else's story. It was like Pandora's box. I hated myself for how good those things made me feel. A door was opening, one that I wasn't sure I would be strong enough to ever go through no matter how desperately I wanted to.

These new thoughts flooded my mind and heart with excitement and fear. I turned to the Internet for more information. I found more and more people like me; transguys, brave men and boys whose stories sounded a lot like mine. I felt torn because I couldn't get enough information, but at the same time, the more I learned, the harder it was for me to deal with what I was realizing about myself. There was no turning back.

One night I went by myself to Wal-Mart and grabbed a package of men's Hanes briefs, opened it up and stuffed a pair into my coat pocket. I have no idea what I would have done if I'd ever been caught, but I knew there was no way I was going to be able to bring them up to the register, at least not then. I got back to my dorm room and locked the door, pulled the shades, and turned my music on loud. I put them on and stood there for a minute taking it in. The thick white cotton felt so right, so much better than plain Hanes Her Ways or even the boxers that I usually wore. Almost without thinking, I opened my underwear drawer and took out a pair of gym socks, rolled one into a ball and stuffed it into my new briefs. I stood up on a chair so I could see myself in the mirror on the wall. It was exhilarating to be doing something that seemed so forbidden but made me feel so complete. I turned to each side, checking out my package in the mirror and feeling it in my hands. I probably stood on that chair for three minutes before getting down and putting on some nice khakis, a men's dress shirt, leather shoes and belt, and a tie. I wore the tightest sports bra I had and went to the bathroom to put gel in my hair. I spent that night alone in my dorm room listening to music and reading. Every once in a while I would move and feel a shift in my pants and that rush would come back to me as I remembered what I had down there.

(continued)

111

PERSONAL REFLECTION: "GROWING UP QUEER" BY KAEL PARKER (*continued*)

Since then, I've had other similar experiences, like the day I bought my first binder, a six-inch-wide Ace bandage from the drugstore. I was so excited to try it out that I stopped in a thrift store and put it on in the dressing room because I couldn't even make it all the way home. I wrapped it around myself as tightly as I could and I almost cried when I looked in the mirror and saw my shirt actually fitting the way I had pictured it when I chose it off the rack, nice and flat against my chest. As I walked out of the store paranoid that the women at the counter would notice the difference in me, I felt about 3,000 times better about myself than I had just ten minutes before. I wasn't feeling quite so good by the time I got home though, I could hardly breathe because it hurt to take in air. I quickly learned my first lesson about binding too tightly.

It was like I had to grow up all over again and learn how to live as a new person, as a transguy. There were a lot more "firsts"; first time shaving my face, first trip to a "real" barber shop, first time buying a suit. But I still look back at that night in my dorm room with the stolen underwear as the beginning of what has been, and is going to be, a long road of self-discovery.

I'm not ashamed anymore of who I am. I have friends who support me and a family that is trying to understand what's happening to their "little girl." I work as an activist for transfolks and other queer youth, sharing my story with as many people as I can. Through exploring and understanding my trans self, my mind has been opened to ideas and people that I hadn't even heard of before. I've made connections and friendships that I hope I never lose.

The hardest thing for me to deal with is knowing that my family will never really see me as their son, and that I will miss out on many things that should be special experiences with them. My father will never stand beside me on my wedding day and wish me luck with my new family or tell me that he is proud of me for becoming an honest and confident young man. My mother will not see the importance of the work I do in the GLBT community because she can't get past her own discomfort with who I am.

Those are some things I've had to give up in order to be true to myself in other parts of my life. It might not be the easiest path, but if I could sit with my father watching a thunderstorm on my front steps tonight, I would tell him that I don't wish I had been "born a boy" and that I am proud to be a strong transman.

even afraid. If you are preparing to transition, make arrangements with your school or place of employment to have safe havens. Some restrooms might become off-limits—to either the person in transition or to her or his colleagues—in order to provide comfortable facilities for all. Prepare peers and colleagues before making a complete transition.

MAKING THE CHANGE

As stated previously, people change along a continuum, hopefully to whatever degree the person is comfortable, but this may be limited to the change a person can financially afford. Hairstyle changes and makeup can start the process. At the same time, anyone attempting such a transition must of necessity become a student of human behavior, observing the ways in which people speak (tone of voice, volume, choice of words, even how they cough or clear their throat), how they move (their body carriage, the purposefulness of each step, even hand gestures), and how they interact. People act differently around persons of the opposite sex than with their own gender. Tutors and coaches are available, for a fee, to help a person learn new behaviors.

Beyond the expense of a new wardrobe (provided one has even felt comfortable enough to shop for new clothes), how does a person get a body of one sex into the clothing of the other? A woman seeking to pass as a man may find mammary tissue posing an obstacle, but breasts can be bound close-to-flat using anything from a firm sports bra and elastic bandage, to supports used for binding hernias. To enhance the appearance of maleness, a suggestive bulge can be created near the crotch of tight-fitting pants using something as simple as a rolled pair of tube socks; this is called *packing*. For a man seeking to pass as a woman, the process must be reversed: pad the bra to create a semblance of breasts and tuck the external genitals into tightly fitted briefs. These, of course, are temporary measures. For a more complete effect, one can take hormones or have surgery—but both require prior medical approval.

Haircuts

Women with short hair who are not taking testosterone generally look different from men with short hair. A good barber can create a convincing haircut, but sideburns must grow in (or be applied with makeup) to complete the male appearance. Men may find wigs to be a useful tool during transition. After all, hair grows slowly.

Hair Removal

Male-to-female transsexuals must deal with the male tendency to produce excessive hair. While female hormone treatments will reduce the amount of body hair, facial hair is not affected. Shaving can provide a temporary fix, but electrolysis is better because it destroys hairs at the root. Mildred L. Brown and Chloe Ann Rounsley, the authors of *True Selves: Understanding Transexualism*, estimate that an average male has at least 30,000 thick facial hairs, which may require 300–500 hours of treatment. Not only is the process tedious and painful, but it may cost as much as the SRS itself.[2]

Voice

Although estrogen does not effect the pitch of a man's voice, testosterone does lower the register of a woman's voice by thickening the vocal cords. Male-to-female (MTF) transsexuals, then, may need to search out voice coaches more often than will their female-to-male (FTM) counterparts.

Chests and Breasts—Nonsurgical Techniques

Pretestosterone FTMs likely will have greater breast development than desired. Chest binding can provide a convincing male silhouette, but it also requires that upper-body clothing be worn throughout the day—even on those hot summer days when other males may wear just an undershirt, if that. While sports bras with a high lycra content are said to provide good compression, undershirts made for biological

Figure 7.2.   Kael Parker, age 20. Male or female?

males with gynecomastia (female-type breast development) are designed specifically for the job. Also, neoprene waist-trimming devices can be used.[3] Elastic bandages can bind the chest more tightly, but the thinner the bandage, the higher the likelihood it will bite painfully into the skin. Before beginning, one should research all the options. This can be done by using medical supply or sporting goods catalogs, or online at sites such as Kael's Page (http://kpscapes.tripod.com).

Resources for the MTF transsexual can be pursued through outlets for the trans community or those designed for female mastectomy patients. Well before considering surgery, options include padding a bra or wearing false breasts inserted into a bra. Under no circumstances should one consider injecting silicone under the skin, as the results can be disastrous. (See the section on silicone below.)

Packing

In order to pass successfully in public, FTM trans persons may choose to "pack" their pants with stuffing to create a bulge suggestive of a penis. (In the opening scene of *Boys Don't Cry*, Hilary Swank's character is preparing to become Brandon. She is seen packing a rolled pair of sweat socks into the front of the jeans she's wearing that night.) Those who seek greater realism can find any number of imitations available in adult stores, up to and including prosthetic penises. Resources for FTM trans people can be found online and through magazine advertisements and stores of various transgender organizations.

Restroom Survival

A woman accustomed to the individual stalls in most public toilets for women may find facing a row of open urinals daunting. Even if she can enjoy the privacy of an individual stall, there is still the matter of the position of feet: when one sits on the toilet (facing forward), the feet are in the opposite position from one who stands to urinate (facing the wall). FTM transsexuals must manage this disparity in a believable fashion. As individual restrooms are not always available, some trans men have developed homemade devices to help channel the flow of urine, allowing a body with female genitals to convincingly make use of men's room facilities. Also, devices marketed to women for use when camping or traveling can be found online and through some sporting goods stores.

Silicone

People seeking to enhance their bodily curves, whether the goal is fuller cheeks or the development of breast tissue, may consider silicone injections; however, a medical advisory on the Gender Education and Advocacy website, Gender.Org, warns against the practice. Injecting silicone into the body, while it may produce quick and pleasing results, can be exceedingly problematic, even life-threatening. In the United States, physicians are prohibited by law from injecting medical-grade silicone into the human body.

People seeking the quick results of silicone may resort to using an underground network of nonmedical personnel who pump industrial-grade silicone (such as that used in caulking compounds, found in hardware and auto parts stores) under the skin for a sizeable fee. A single treatment may cost a few hundred dollars, and multiple treatments are often required to get the desired result. Providers that skip into and out of town quickly enough to avoid detection by authorities leave their clients to their own devices should complications ensue—and some complications may not arise for years.

One hazard with silicone injections is acute respiratory distress, which can occur several years after the injection itself. Another hazard is that silicone may soften and move within the body, causing lumps and bumps in undesirable locations. Once silicone is introduced into the body, it can be difficult to remove; people who have had silicone injected to enlarge breast tissue sometimes require a mastectomy (removal of the entire breast) to get rid of it later. Anyone seeking to make permanent changes to his or her appearance is urged to carefully research both the procedure and the provider before acting.[4]

Hormone Treatments

After working with a gender therapist for a number of months (three or six to start), a transsexual may be deemed ready to undertake hormone treatments.[5] The introduction of male or female hormones to the body causes distinct changes.

HORMONES ARE STRONG MEDICINES, AND SHOULD BE RESPECTED IF YOU DECIDE TO TAKE THEM

Figure 7.3. Preparing to take hormones, Garret, Grant, and Tera use caution.

According to the Harry Benjamin Standards of Care (see below), hormones should be used with caution, under a physician's supervision, and only in persons no younger than 18 years old.

Testosterone

For the FTM transsexual, testosterone injections cause a number of changes. Those listed in Brown and Rounsley's *True Selves* include the following:

- thickening of vocal cords and a deepening of the voice
- increased growth of facial and body hair
- increased mass and strength of muscles
- cessation of menstruation and ovulation
- coarsening and increasing oiliness of skin
- appearance or increase of acne
- redistribution of body fat to slim hips and waist with no reduction of breast size
- increase of libidinal drive
- thinning of hair and development of male pattern-baldness (if inherited)

Notice how Kael Parker's appearance in figure 7.4, following hormone treatment, has changed from that of the earlier photos. The girl in figures 5.3 and 5.4 has vanished, replaced by a muscular young man with sideburns.

Figure 7.4.   Kael Parker, age 23. Notice how testosterone has created a distinctly masculine appearance.

Estrogen

For the MTF transsexual, estrogen can be taken by injections, pills, or skin patches. It generally causes a number of changes. Those listed in *True Selves* include the following:

- lessening of body hair
- growth of breasts
- decreased mass and strength of muscles
- softening of the skin
- redistribution of body fat, resulting in rounded hips and breasts and a smaller waistline
- decrease of sexual function
- cessation of any male pattern baldness

Hormone treatments include risks and side effects including increased blood pressure, heart or liver disease, and blood clots. Once hormone treatments have been started, they need to be continued throughout a person's life.

Surgeries

Several nongenital cosmetic surgical procedures are available. Some of the more commonly performed surgeries, as reported by Brown and Rounsley, are:

- tracheal shave to reduce the size of a prominent Adam's apple
- rhinoplasty (nose job)
- face-lift
- changing the shape of the forehead
- changing the contour of the chin
- changing the angle of the lower jaw
- acid peel for smoother skin
- hair implants to correct baldness
- cheek implants
- voice surgery to tighten the vocal cords (with varying results)

HORMONES CAN CHANGE APPETITES...

...BUT NOT WHO YOU ARE

Figure 7.5. *Top:* Mikeala (as Allen) eats a burger beside Grant (as Adrianne), who sips a soda. *Bottom:* Mikeala (as herself) now prefers soda beside Grant (as himself), who now eats a burger. Although their appetites have changed, their thoughts remain the same.

Sexual reassignment surgery is major surgery; indeed it may include a number of operations. According to the Harry Benjamin Standards of Care, prerequisites include living full-time in the desired gender for at least one full year. (Figures 7.7 and 7.8 illustrate time lines of the gender transition process.)

Breast reduction (mastectomy) or enhancement is also referred to as "top" surgery. "Bottom" surgery refers to the removal of sex organs and the creation of genitals through plastic surgery. Bottom operations could include hysterectomy, vaginectomy, urethroplasty, and phalloplasty for the FTM transsexual, vaginoplasty and labiaplasty for the MTF transsexual. Although such surgeries do not create internal organs, they can create structures that are similar in appearance to genetic female or male genitalia. Election to undergo SRS is an extremely personal choice.

Surgery can be prohibitively expensive and cost anywhere from tens of thousands of dollars to more than $100,000. Plastic surgery performed for cosmetic reasons is generally not covered by any insurance plan. Some people choose to seek

Figure 7.6.   Mikeala and Tera react individually to the mention of surgery.

treatment overseas. Even with the expense of travel, treatment in some Asian countries may be thousands of dollars less expensive than in the United States.

Beyond the financial cost, persons considering SRS must weigh the risks and benefits. Any surgical procedure carries with it a measure of medical risk. Internal bleeding or postoperative infection can be a life-threatening complication. No one undergoes SRS without first undertaking extensive and time-consuming preparations.

Legal Changes

At the beginning of the real-life experience of living full-time in the opposite gender role, various legal hurdles present themselves. Most people assume a new name in addition to the new gender, and these changes require revisions to existing legal documents. A multitude of documents require changes, including one's driver's license, social security card, credit cards and bank accounts, employment and school records, titles and deeds to property, professional licenses and credentials, patents, will, stocks or bonds, and passport. Laws regarding changes to birth certificates vary from state to state. In addition, the Real ID Act of 2005, enacted in May of that year, gave states three years to issue "licenses and identification cards with an eight-year validity period that contains machine-readable technology" and to maintain a corresponding database.[6] Accomplishing all of these changes is a daunting task that is both time-consuming and often frustrating. In the process, transsexuals must take care not to obliterate all past records, as sometimes they might need to prove their prior identities.[7]

Needless to say, each of the steps involved in a gender transition requires emotional strength and fortitude. In obtaining a diagnosis of Gender Identity Disorder, a person becomes a mental health patient, a fact which may impede future access to some types of insurance. No one should undertake such a change lightly.

THE HARRY BENJAMIN STANDARDS OF CARE

The Harry Benjamin International Gender Dysphoria Association (HBIGDA) established standards of care in 1977 that have been regularly updated since their inception. These standards provide prerequisites to hormone treatments or sexual reassignment surgery (SRS). Although the effects of female hormones on MTF transsexuals are usually reversible, the effects of male hormones on FTM transsexuals can be permanent. The standards call for a gender therapist to work with a client at least three months before beginning hormone treatment; however, most HBIGDA therapists wait six months before starting FTM hormone treatments. Prior to approval of SRS, therapists adhering to these standards require the "real-life test" (RLT) or "real-life experience" (RLE). This requires a person to live full-time, twenty-four hours a day, seven days a week, for a full year as a member of the gender to which he or she wishes to switch before being approved for surgery.

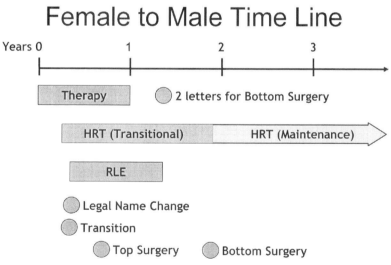

Figure 7.7.   Timeline for transition from female to male. Therapy—including a diagnosis of gender identity disorder—transitional hormone treatment (HRT), and a real-life experience (RLE) are all prerequisites to sexual reassignment surgery (SRS). Before undergoing "bottom" surgery, the FTM transsexual must also obtain two letters of support from professionals in the field. *(Mary Ann Horton, Ph.D., Red Ace Consulting Services)*

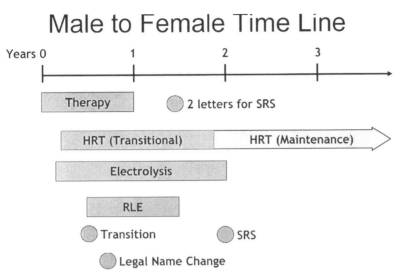

Male to Female Time Line

Figure 7.8.   Timeline for transition from male to female. Therapy—
including a diagnosis of gender identity disorder—two letters of
support from professionals in the field, transitional hormone
treatment (HRT), electrolysis, and a real-life experience (RLE) are all
prerequisites to MTF sexual reassignment surgery. *(Mary Ann Horton,
Ph.D., Red Ace Consulting Services)*

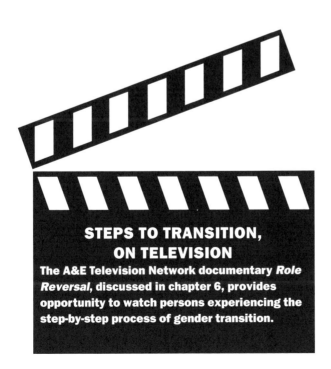

**STEPS TO TRANSITION,
ON TELEVISION**

The A&E Television Network documentary *Role
Reversal*, discussed in chapter 6, provides
opportunity to watch persons experiencing the
step-by-step process of gender transition.

Although some patients find the RLT process cumbersome, the standards help ensure that only appropriate individuals are approved for such treatments.[8]

NOTES

1. William Shakespeare, *The Tragedy of Hamlet, Prince of Denmark*, act 1, scene 3, lines 78–80, in *The Norton Shakespeare* (New York: Norton, 1997).

2. Mildred L. Brown and Chloe Ann Rounsley, *True Selves: Understanding Transsexualism . . . for Families, Friends, Coworkers, and Helping Professionals* (San Francisco: Jossey-Bass, 1996), 134.

3. Neoprene is a synthetic rubber used for specialized clothing such as gloves or wetsuits.

4. Dallas Denny's article "Dangerous Curves Ahead" outlines the short-term benefits and long-term pitfalls of silicone injections and includes vignettes of persons who later experienced complications; *TS–TV Tapestry*, no. 61 (1992), available at www.gender.org/resources/bad_news.html.

5. The sections on hormone treatments and surgeries draw heavily from "Medical and Surgical Options," in Brown and Rounsley, *True Selves*, 196–211.

6. Melissa A. Savage, "Real ID Update," National Conference of State Legislatures, April 2006, www.ncsl.org/programs/transportation/RealIDupdate06.htm.

7. Brown and Rounsley, *True Selves*, 130–31.

8. Brown and Rounsley, *True Selves*, 101–3.

The Law Today

HELPING PEOPLE UNDER-
STAND GENDER ISSUES
HELPS YOU, TOO

If you look around—in school, at the mall, at a park—you may be aware of varied gender expressions: the girl with a buzz cut, the boy who is more effeminate than macho. But for the most part, everyone (including the two aforementioned individuals) will look relatively normal to you. Why is that? For one thing, we're living in the twenty-first century, where diversity is often expressed and even celebrated. Today's women and men have far more socially accepted ways of expressing themselves and their gender than did our forebears. Think about it. Can you imagine life before blue jeans? Can you imagine being female before women wore pants?

Although today's women wear pants, run for public office and vote, and enter careers as a matter of course, legal protections for sexual minorities and gender-variant individuals have much room for improvement. During the time this book was being written, laws concerning gender issues have evolved, and they continue to do so today. When the state of Massachusetts broke

ARRESTED FOR WEARING PANTS

Cross-dressing was once illegal. In August 1915, the *Chicago Daily News* published a photograph of a Mrs. Anna Roseman with the explanation that she had been arrested and fined $100 because she was wearing men's clothing! After that, she was sent to the Erring Women's Refuge in Chicago.

the marriage barrier for same-sex couples, a huge legal victory for gay rights was realized. By legalizing same-sex marriage, the state granted equal status to unions that many had never expected to be sanctioned by law. At the same time, the action in Massachusetts served to strengthen the resolve of people and groups who believe gender-variant individuals should not have "special" rights and should not be treated equally in the eyes of the law or society. As the fight to repeal the same-sex marriage law continues in Massachusetts, other states are giving serious consideration to their own laws. Not only did President George W. Bush campaign for reelection speaking out against same-sex marriage and proposing an amendment be written into the United States Constitution to that effect, but the 2004 presidential election also coincided with the passage of more than a dozen state antigay marriage amendments and ballot initiatives.

Figure 8.1. If witnessing a person's change of gender presentation seems challenging for the outsider, just imagine the roadblocks faced by the person in transition. Present-day laws protect the person in transition far more than they did a hundred years ago. Here, Tera faces an imagined scene of opposition to her changes.

THE EVOLUTION OF MARRIAGE RIGHTS

While the first of the antimiscegenation[1] laws to be struck down was California's in 1948, as recently as 2000 it was still illegal for interracial couples to marry in some states. As people of color have been granted equal status in the eyes of the law, sexual minorities have lagged far behind in the fight for their rights.

In 1993 the Hawaii Supreme Court ruled (in *Baehr v. Lewin*) that it was illegal for the state to deny same-sex couples marriage licenses. This created such a backlash that President Bill Clinton signed the federal Defense of Marriage Act (DOMA) in 1996 stating that marriage is only legal between one man and one woman. Later, in 1998, ballot initiatives were passed in both Hawaii and Alaska to the same effect.

The Vermont legislature established civil unions after a 1999 ruling by the Vermont Supreme Court that same-sex couples be allowed the rights and benefits of marriage. By establishing civil unions, the legislature continued to maintain that marriage can occur only between a man and a woman, but created a parallel set of rights and benefits for same-sex couples. Connecticut, in 2005, became the second state to approve same-sex civil unions.

In 2004 Massachusetts became the first state in the union to grant full marriage rights to same-sex couples after the Massachusetts Supreme Judicial Court (*Goodridge et al. v. Department of Public Health et al.*) ruled that individuals have a constitutional right to marry the person of one's choice. Although the repercussions included moves in 2004 and 2005 to amend the Massachusetts constitution to define marriage as a union between one man and one woman, the November 2004 elections saw every incumbent who supported equal marriage rights reelected and a number of anti-equality incumbents unseated. As this book goes to press, active attempts to place a ballot question before the voters in 2008 to define marriage as between a man and a woman continue.

Interestingly, a Massachusetts law passed in 1913—making marriages in Massachusetts illegal for couples residing outside the state for whom marriage would be illegal in their home states—was dusted off and again enforced in 2004. While the original law kept interracial couples residing in states with antimiscegenation laws from marrying in Massachusetts, in

(*continued*)

THE EVOLUTION OF MARRIAGE RIGHTS (*continued*)

2004 it was used to prevent marriages of same-sex couples residing in states with laws defining marriage as the union between a man and a woman.

Presently, federal marriage rights remain unavailable for homosexual couples, and the political and social struggles continue. With passionate and articulate advocates on both sides of the issue, the issue will continue to be hotly debated.

SAFE SCHOOLS

What rights do you feel gender-variant individuals should have? Should "all men are created equal" really mean that all *people* are created equal—and deserve equal protection in the eyes of the law? Think about it. Each time a minority or oppressed class of persons is granted an "equal" right, then the majority or ruling class effectively loses some special treatment previously accorded them. When *Brown v. Board of Education*,[2] decided that "segregation of white and Negro children in the public schools of a State solely on the basis of race . . . denies to Negro children the equal protection of the laws guaranteed by the Fourteenth Amendment" and that Negro children must "be admitted to the white schools because of their superiority to the Negro schools," then the privileged white students lost their right to have racially separate schools. Although it is true that we all gain something by having culturally diverse learning environments, those formerly at the top lost their exclusive privilege to have the best education that could be offered in a culturally homogeneous learning environment.

We have come a long way since *Brown vs. Board of Education*, far enough that to some people the suggestion that racially separate but equal schools might be considered again may seem ludicrous. At the same time, socioeconomic factors continue to enable wealthier communities (where people in power tend to live) to provide their schools with better quality facilities and materials than poor communities (where disadvantaged and oppressed people tend to live) can provide. What should be done to improve educational equality across schools while providing every student with the best possible education?

One aspect of educational equality that is often overlooked involves students' right to protection from harm while at school. Gender-variant (lesbian, gay, bisexual, and transgender) students need to have their rights stated in the law in order for them to realize protections equal to those of their peers while in school. In 1993, Massachusetts became the first state to enact a "safe schools" law. Laws like this give all students, including those who are gender-variant, the right to feel safe in their educational environment and make it illegal to harass and intimidate those who are perceived as being different with regard to sex or sexual orientation. Without these laws, intimidating someone by scrawling "queer" across his or her locker might be perceived by some as morally wrong, but it wouldn't be illegal. Even with safe schools laws in place and a supportive faculty and staff, LGBT students, who often face teasing and harassment in schools, must advocate for themselves.

Even before the advent of safe schools laws, New York City's consideration of school safety for LGBT youth became clear with the opening of the Harvey Milk High School in 1985. Named for San Francisco's openly gay City Supervisor Harvey Milk, who was slain at City Hall in 1978, Milk High School began as a two-room alternative program designed to provide a safe haven for the most at-risk gay students who had been harassed in other school settings. A cooperative effort between the Hetrick-Martin Institute and the New York Department of Education, the world's first gay school program quietly helped students for nearly twenty years. But when the school opened as a distinctly separate building in 2003, it quickly became controversial. Although the school is technically open to all students, opponents argue that federal and state tax dollars should not be "used to fund a segregated high school for homosexual students."[3] When it was targeted as a segregationist school providing special services to LGBT youth, Milk High School was defended by advocates for LGBT youth, including New York City mayor Michael Bloomberg. Since its inception in 1985, other school programs have been modeled after Harvey Milk High.

In Washington State, the Safe Schools Initiative has strong backing in the Department of Education. Eighty-six percent of the Washington State school districts that participated in a 2003 survey identified "gender identity" as a distinguishing characteristic included in their policies against harassment, intimidation, and bullying (HIB). The state's "Bullying Report" compares the 2003 responses to those responses given the prior year, just after Substitute House Bill 1444, the Anti-Bullying Act, was signed into law. The results show that Washington State schools expanded their categories of prohibited HIB acts during the intervening year and that school districts were working hard to inform their professional staff of current HIB policies and to provide staff training. Further, many districts have incorporated antibullying curricula into their programs, working to inform students and to keep schools safe for all students.[4]

Federal and state laws mandate that schools provide safe spaces for students to learn. Some state policies specifically address sexual orientation or gender identity. To see if your state has included these characteristics, or to find guidelines for forming safe schools policies, consult the Safe Schools Coalition, Transgender Law and Policy Institute (TLPI), or American Civil Liberties Union (ACLU). Feeling unsafe at school (and elsewhere) can be a frightening, isolating

SAFE SCHOOLS LAW

In response to a 1993 education report, "Making Schools Safe for Gay and Lesbian Youth: Breaking the Silence in Schools and in Families," issued by the Massachusetts Governor's Commission on Gay and Lesbian Youth, and extensive personal testimony by gay and lesbian adolescents before the state legislature, Massachusetts Governor William Weld signed a law deeming that schools must be kept safe for GLBT youth.

> **SAFE COLLEGES AND UNIVERSITIES**
>
> As of July 2006, the Transgender Law and Policy Institute listed sixty-eight colleges and universities and two law schools on its website (http://www.transgenderlaw.org/college) whose nondiscrimination policies include gender identity and expression, and seven others with some form of gender identity/expression protection or that are considering adding gender identity/expression to their nondiscrimination policies. Also listed are schools that:
>
> - require or encourage staff to attend training on transgender issues
> - provide for the health care needs of transgender students
> - offer gender-neutral residence halls and other mixed-gender housing options
> - provide gender-neutral restrooms and unisex changing facilities
> - provide options beyond "male" and "female" when requesting students identify gender on forms
> - have locker room facilities that are private or offer individual, curtained shower stalls

experience. Even with student and faculty support, homo- and transphobic taunts and jibes hurled in your direction can undermine the climate of safety. If you feel unsafe in your school, find out what the law requires in your location and what is school policy, then seek moral support from a trusted adult. Use the resources above, or contact another agency specializing in antidiscrimination such as your local Human Rights Commission, Gay and Lesbian Advocates and Defenders (GLAD), National Center for Lesbian Rights (NCLR), or Southern Poverty Law Center (SPLC). Finding a voice of support, no matter how far away, is a valuable step.

ANTIDISCRIMINATION LAWS

In March 2005, Maine became the sixth state—following Minnesota (1993), Rhode Island (2001), New Mexico and

California (2003), and Illinois (2005)—to include gender identity and expression in its antidiscrimination laws. At that time, TLPI also reported ten counties and sixty-one cities across the United States that have policies or laws prohibiting discrimination on the basis of gender or sexual

DAY OF SILENCE

Together, the Gay, Lesbian, and Straight Education Network (GLSEN) and United States Student Association (USSA) sponsor an annual day of student-led action when supporters of making anti-LGBT bias unacceptable in schools take a daylong vow of silence in support of those LGBT students and their allies who have effectively been silenced by oppression. On April 26, 2006, the project reported that an estimated 500,000 students at 4,000 schools in every state, the District of Columbia, and Puerto Rico made the tenth annual Day of Silence the largest single-day, student-led action on LGBT issues in history. Visit www.dayofsilence.org for more information.

orientation. Eighty-seven years after Mrs. Anna Roseman was arrested in 1915 for wearing pants, the city of Chicago updated its antidiscrimination laws to include gender identity as a protected characteristic.

In a time when political correctness, if not actual laws, may prevent people who discriminate from stating their reasons for doing so, determining whether one has experienced discrimination may not be easy. A prospective employer is not likely to say, "We don't hire transgender persons here," and a prospective landlord is not likely to say, "We don't want your kind living here" (whatever "your kind" may be). Even so, it is important to know what laws are available to protect you. For example, while the First Amendment guarantees that anyone has the right to join a LGBT organization, it does not stop private employers from choosing to forgo hiring someone based on that association.

One setting where LGBT discrimination is not only legal but even exists as written policy is the military. U.S. military policy states that "homosexuality is incompatible with military service." For years, simply the suspicion that a servicemember was gay or lesbian could trigger a full-scale investigation, akin to the "witch hunts" of old. Military recruits were directly asked about their sexual orientation. Servicemembers under suspicion were investigated, prosecuted, and possibly threatened with court-martial or imprisonment unless they provided names of other homosexual or bisexual servicemembers. Then, in his 1992 presidential campaign, Bill Clinton stated that he opposed the military exclusion of GLBT

CABLE DOCUMENTARY: "TRANSGENDER REVOLUTION"

The Point, an A&E Television Network program, aired the episode "Transgender Revolution" in 2002, examining transsexuals and gender oppression. Beginning with the profile of an FTM law enforcement officer, "Transgender Revolution" examines one person's experience with on-the-job discrimination and how he chose to fight it. The next segment profiles the MTF host of the weekly GenderTalk Radio show and what she has done to make transgender issues visible to the world. Then a transsexual explains the need to go beyond living as a man to having sexual reassignment surgery, and how the surgery will enable the individual to attain the legal identification and rights of a male.

Viewers are exposed to the concept of the next revolution being gender based and are asked if America is ready for a transgender revolution.

persons. In 1993, President Clinton's "Don't Ask, Don't Tell, Don't Pursue, Don't Harass" policy was enacted. Although GLBT persons are still unable to serve openly, Clinton's measure prevents servicepersons and recruits from being *asked* about their sexuality. Further, it discourages disclosures; a serviceperson who admits to being gay is still discharged from military service. "Don't pursue" put a stop to the witch hunts, and "don't harass" was designed to stop intimidation and harassment on the basis of sexual orientation.[5] Between 1994 and 2005, at least 600 service members were discharged each year under "Don't Ask, Don't Tell."[6]

With regard to employment in the private sector, LGBT discrimination may be legal where no law exists specifically protecting persons on the basis of sexual orientation, gender identity, or gender expression. Even where such laws do exist, they may offer only limited protection. For example, employers may not be allowed to discriminate in hiring practices, but they may very well discriminate in terms of benefits offered. Sometimes married couples may be entitled to insurance benefits while domestic partners are not. Although the legal scaffolding for gender identity and expression at work is still developing, the Human Rights Campaign (HRC) project WorkNet has noted significant positive growth in recent years as more Fortune 500 companies and hundreds of public and private employers have added gender identity to their nondiscrimination policies.[7] As the laws and practices continue to evolve, one may be best served by consulting an organization such as the ACLU, Gay & Lesbian Advocates and Defenders (GLAD), or Transgender At Work (TAW) with specific questions.

Housing is another area where gender identity or sexual orientation may be cause for discrimination. When seeking

FINDING A COMPATIBLE EMPLOYER

Are you job hunting? Interested in working for an employer who includes gender identity in its nondiscrimination policy? Consult the HRC WorkNet website (www.hrc.org/worknet) to find which employers have taken this step and explore the possibilities.

housing, one would be well served to know the laws of the state or municipality and to determine to what extent you are willing to fight for your legal rights. Safety at home is of prime concern, which may lead a potential renter to be cautious in exercising her or his rights. If the neighborhood appears welcoming but the rental agent or landlord seems hesitant, it may be the time to assert yourself. For teens still living at home, the issues of sexual orientation and gender identity or expression can be extremely volatile. In fact, LGBT youth may account for between 25 and 40 percent of homeless youth on the streets today.[8]

HATE CRIMES LAWS

Acts of discrimination offer many ways of communicating one's displeasure with a group or class of people, and while discriminatory practices can be extremely hurtful, they are rarely lethal. Hate crimes are in another class. They offer perpetrators violent avenues for expression of their hatred.

Before the turn of the twenty-first century, only four states included gender in their hate crimes laws. Minnesota (in 1988), California (1998), and Missouri and Vermont (1999) all saw fit to protect transgender individuals from violent assaults committed against them by perpetrators motivated by hate for the victim's gender or gender expression. In 2000, the city of Ithaca, New York, became the first city to include gender in its hate crime law. By 2004, Pennsylvania, New Mexico, Hawaii, and Connecticut had added gender to the list of protected categories of persons.[9] That means that, as this book goes to press, in forty-two states, the District of Columbia, and the territory of Puerto Rico, transgender people are not specifically protected by law from hate crimes committed against them. Reaching far beyond basic discrimination, hate crimes involve violent attacks on persons for who they are and may result in severe injury or even death.

In 2005, the U.S. House of Representatives voted to protect transgender persons as part of the Local Law Enforcement Hate Crimes Prevention Act of 2005. This bill is designed to provide local law enforcement agencies with the tools needed to investigate and prosecute hate crimes. The bill defines a hate crime as any willful act of violence resulting in death or bodily injury motivated by the "actual or perceived religion, national origin, gender, sexual orientation, gender identity, or disability." The addition of sexual

CALIFORNIA LAW

California Penal Code section 422.6(a) reads: "No person, whether or not acting under color of law, shall by force or threat of force, willfully injure, intimidate, interfere with, oppress, or threaten any other person in the free exercise or enjoyment of any right or privilege secured to him or her by the Constitution or laws of this state or by the Constitution or laws of the United States because of the other person's race, color, religion, ancestry, national origin, disability, gender, or sexual orientation, or because he or she perceives that the other person has one or more of those characteristics." Gender is included as a protected category throughout sections 422.6–422.95.

orientation and gender to existing federal hate crimes laws has been hotly debated. Those in opposition view the passage of such legislation as approval of the homosexual lifestyle by the federal government.

The legislative process can be excruciatingly slow and complicated, and various forms of this bill have been proposed in Congress each year since the late twentieth century without success. Keep an eye on the news headlines to track the passage of legislation through Congress. Hate crimes committed against persons for their perceived sexual orientation, gender identity, or gender expression can be extremely violent. Although the brutal 1998 murder of Matthew Shepard—a twenty-one-year-

LEGISLATIVE INFORMATION ON THE INTERNET

Interested in the status of a congressional bill? The U.S. government helps anyone with Internet access to track current and past federal legislation through its Thomas website. Named for Thomas Jefferson and provided by the Library of Congress, http://thomas.loc.gov is a user-friendly site that allows anyone to be informed about and participate in the democratic process.

BRANDON TEENA

On Christmas Day 1993, twenty-one-year-old Brandon Teena (born Teena Brandon and the subject of the award-winning film *Boys Don't Cry*) was murdered in a Nebraska farmhouse, in front of a friend and her nine-month-old child. Teena had earlier been beaten and raped by two "friends" who discovered that he was biologically female.[10] Although he reported his rape to the Richardson County sheriff, a deputy was forbidden to arrest his rapists; instead, his attackers were informed of Teena's report. Subsequently, Teena was murdered. Brandon Teena's family waited a long time for justice; in 2001, the Nebraska High Court finally held the county sheriff accountable for the death.[11]

---

old who was beaten and left to die tied to a fencepost in freezing weather in Laramie, Wyoming—brought a wave of media attention to anti-LGBT violence, most of us are unaware of the extent of the problem. Violence against transgender persons can frequently be lethal, as it was in Brandon Teena's case (see sidebar). In fact, an instructor at San Francisco's Harvey Milk Institute estimated that transgender individuals living in America today have a one in twelve chance of being murdered.[12]

After Teena's unfortunate experience with law enforcement, the September 2005 release of a report by Amnesty International USA may be a step in the direction of added safety for LGBT persons who encounter police. The unprecedented report, entitled "Stonewalled: Police Abuse and Misconduct against Lesbian, Gay, Bisexual and Transgender (LGBT) People in the U.S.," is a disturbing indictment of law enforcement in the United States.[13] The report was based on in-depth research, including survivor interviews, police department surveys, and review of "police policies and training in four major cities." One of the report's central conclusions was that "transgender individuals, particularly women and young people, bear the disproportionate brunt of police brutality against LGBT people." However, the advent of the report's disclosures may help to overcome such behavior. One result is that citizen activists across the country are calling for their local police departments to sign Amnesty International's Pledge for

CABLE MOVIE: *A GIRL LIKE ME*

In June 2006 the Lifetime Television original movie *A Girl Like Me: The Gwen Arujo Story* premiered before an audience in excess of 5 million viewers. Based on a true story, *A Girl Like Me* tells the story of a transgender teen whose vicious murder bears remembering. Raised by a single mother, Eddie Arujo received his mother's loving support when he decided in his teens to live as a female. The movie depicts Eddie's transition to Gwen, her murder at the hands of a transphobic group of men, and the subsequent trial. None of her attackers was convicted of perpetrating a hate crime, although murder and manslaughter convictions were forthcoming. Sentences fifteen years to life were handed down with the murder convictions; the manslaughter conviction carried a six-year sentence. *A Girl Like Me* effectively portrays the anguish experienced by Gwen's family owing to transphobia.

Professionalism. Further, the report's release coincided with the historic House of Representatives vote to add gender and gender identity to federal hate crimes laws, and the Atlanta Police Department's dismissal of an officer for antigay verbal abuse. Taken together, these may be indicators that transgender and LGB people are garnering more notice and respect in our society.

NOTES

1. *Miscegenation* is intermarriage (or "cross-breeding") between races. Antimiscegenation laws, making interracial marriage illegal,

were passed in the United States to discourage mixed-race relationships between blacks and whites.

2. *Brown v. Board of Education*, 347 U.S. 483 (1954) (USSC+), opinion delivered by Mr. Chief Justice Warren for the Supreme Court of the United States, 17 May 1954, www.nationalcenter.org/brown.html.

3. Randy Hedlund, "Segregation by Any Other Name: Harvey Milk High School," *Journal of Law and Education* (2004 July).

4. Lauren Hafner, "Bullying Report: How Are Washington State Schools Doing?" December 2003, www.safeschoolscoalition.org/bullyreport/bullyreport12-03.html.

5. This paragraph draws from Human Rights Campaign, "Don't Ask, Don't Tell, Don't Pursue, Don't Harass," http://www.hrc.org/content/navigationmenu/hrc/get_informed/issues.

6. Servicemembers Legal Defense Network (SLDN), "Annual 'Don't Ask, Don't Tell' Dismissals, 1994–2005," www.sldn.org/binary-data/sldn_articles/pdf_file/1455.pdf.

7. "Has corporate America protected the transgender community?" in Transgender Basics, Human Rights Campaign (2004). www.hrc.org/Content/NavigationMenu/HRC/Get_Informed/Issues/Transgender_Issues1/ Transgender_Basics/Transgender_Basics.htm.

8. Safe Schools Coalition, "Homeless LGBT Youth and LGBT Youth in Foster Care," www.safeschoolscoalition.org/rg-homeless.html#statistics.

9. Transgender Law and Policy Institute, "Jurisdictions with Transgender-Inclusive Hate Crimes Laws," www.transgenderlaw.org/hatecrimelaws/index.htm.

10. Human Rights Campaign, "Transgender Basics," 2004, www.hrc.org/content/navigationmenu/hrc/get_informed/issues/transgender_issues1/transgender_basics/transgender_basics.htm.

11. "Nebraska's Highest Court Unanimously Holds Sheriff Accountable for Brandon Teena's Death," Lambda Legal Defense and Education Fund, press release, 20 April 2001, www.lambdalegal.org/cgi-bin/iowa/documents/record?record=825.

12. Kay Brown, *Washington Blade*, 10 December 1999, cited in Human Rights Campaign, "Transgender Basics," 2004, www.hrc.org/content/navigationmenu/hrc/get_informed/issues/transgender_issues1/transgender_basics/transgender_basics.htm.

13. This section is based on Walter Armstrong, "Brutality in Blue," *Amnesty Magazine*, Winter 2005, 17–19; quotes are drawn from Armstrong's article.

How You Can Make a Difference

Now that you've educated yourself about the intricacies of gender, how can you make a difference in the world? First and foremost, speak out! Breaking the silence around such taboo topics as intersex children, or trans persons' positions on the broad spectrum of gender identity and expression, is necessary in order to normalize their existence—and clearly trans and intersex persons are everywhere. In biology classrooms, ask about chromosomal structures beyond XX and XY. Your teacher may not feel prepared to teach information outside the norm, but appeal to his or her scientific curiosity. You could ask for extra credit and offer to bring information in yourself; by providing information about the Intersex Society of North America (ISNA) to your science teacher, you are educating a person who will, in turn, educate many others through the years. In health classrooms, ask questions that encourage inquiry into and discussions about the multifaceted nature of gender identity and expression (and sexual orientation, if your teacher is willing to tackle it) and the possibility that they exist on a broad spectrum, not just the duality of male/female or the categories of heterosexual/bisexual/homosexual.

Some readers may be too young to recall when the AIDS activist group ACT UP (the AIDS Coalition to Unleash Power) first brought out Keith Haring posters proclaiming "Silence = Death." The reasoning behind the equation was that by maintaining silence around difficult or taboo sexual topics, the spread of HIV (the virus that causes AIDS) would continue, permitting the AIDS epidemic to flourish and people to die. If people would discuss their HIV status or risks before becoming sexual partners, unnecessary deaths could be averted. In a similar way, intersex individuals who have suffered at the hands of the medical establishment (albeit when doctors were seeking to improve the person's life circumstances through normalization) realize that society's continued silence about intersex conditions will result in the death of sexual pleasure or other problems for many more individuals. Remember that some five clitorectomies are performed daily in the United States on infant girls with clitorises larger than three-eighths of an inch! Americans express outrage about female circumcisions routinely practiced by other cultures, but remain mute about the treatment of intersex infants here in the United States. Change that by breaking the silence.

ARTIST AS ACTIVIST

Keith Haring (1958–1990), the visual artist who created the "Silence = Death" posters for ACT UP, made a huge impact on our society during his short life. An American painter, Haring's line figures and bold colors readily catch the eye, inviting the mind to go further. Visit the Keith Haring website at www.haring.com for more information, examples of his work, and a link to the Keith Haring/Pop Shop of New York.

The full ACT UP slogan was "Knowledge = Power; Silence = Death" for good reason. People discuss what they know. We learn from these discussions. Armed with knowledge, persons can make intelligent decisions and effect change upon their lives and communities. The treatment of intersex conditions as medical emergencies serves only to preserve the silence of taboo topics. Concerned physicians seeking to make newborns "normal" are—in the eyes of some who have experienced such "care"—depriving the individuals from making informed decisions about their own bodies and their futures as sexual beings. ISNA was formed in opposition to this standard of care, and it seeks to educate the medical community about the consequences of early surgery and the benefits of alternative

Figure 9.1. Mikeala speaks about trans issues.

treatment models. Surgery for children with genital abnormalities is no longer automatic, and parents are included in the decision making. Some medical centers now make a point to consult psychologists and other experts such as pediatric urologists in these complex intersex cases, and some medical schools are teaching alternatives to early genital surgery.[1] An informed public has the power to make intelligent decisions. Speak out to ensure that the existence of intersex conditions and their relative frequency of occurrence is understood in your community.

Other places to speak out include social science (history) and language arts (English) classrooms. Make statements and ask questions about the power of language. Introduce your teachers to the Teaching Tolerance campaign of the Southern Poverty Law Center (SPLC), which is dedicated to providing free curriculum materials for teachers. Introduce your peers to Mix It Up, the SPLC resource for student activists. The website, Tolerance.org, provides curriculum materials, including *The Power of Words* and *Writing for Change*.[2] With lesson plans and handouts developed for elementary, secondary, and college students, teachers can enrich their curricula. By introducing teachers to these materials (or renewing their interest in them), you will definitely make a difference. Remember, education is a powerful tool. You serve your community by making others aware of the existence of intersex conditions; of the differences among gender roles, identity and expression, physical or biological sex, and sexual orientation; and of the power language has to influence the world. Armed with such knowledge, each person is better prepared to decide for him- or herself what stance to take on these issues.

As always, watch your language. Be inclusive. Avoid the rigid M/F and G/L/B categories alone and include "intersex" and "trans" in your working vocabulary. Of course, almost no one can, or wants to be, politically correct 100 percent of the time. Policing our own language can be tiring and may even strain friendships. But simply being aware of the words you speak and hear, and choosing your own words with care (or correcting yourself when you hear that you've misspoken), will effect change in the world around you.

SCHOLARSHIP OPPORTUNITY

The International Foundation for Gender Education (IFGE) provides scholarships through its collaborative Transgender Scholarship and Education Legacy Fund (TSELF). TSELF scholarships are available for "out and proud" transgender students of any age for postsecondary educational needs in the helping and caring professions in the United States or Canada. Each scholarship will provide supplemental funding for postsecondary students who have a demonstrated ability in and commitment to affecting change in the transgender communities through their decision to work and become educated in the helping and caring professions. These include, but are not limited to, social services, health care, religious instruction (all denominations), teaching, and the law.

Complete information and applications may be found at www.tself.org or through the IFGE website at www.ifge.org. In addition, you may contact TSELF directly at the International Foundation for Gender Education, TSELF Awards Committee, P.O. Box 540229, Waltham, MA 02454-0229.

START A GSA

Does your school have a Gay–Straight Alliance? A place where students of all persuasions—gay, straight, bisexual, intersex, queer, transsexual, and questioning—can meet and share ideas safely, can open doors for so many people. Before you begin, realize that having a GSA does not mean that your school

CAMPUS RESOURCE

The GSA Network has developed an entire curriculum to reduce the use of intolerant language on campus. This ready-made course is available in its publication *Take It Back: A Manual for Fighting Slurs on Campus*, which you can find at www.gsanetwork.org.

promotes homosexuality, heterosexuality, or sexual activity of any kind. It does mean, however, that your school and its administration support schools being centers of education, where open minds can gain valuable information and where students can question the order of the universe. Through this process of listening and questioning in a safe space, people grow to be healthy, thinking citizens, ready to take action (large or small) in their communities.

CAMPUS ACTIVISM

College and university campuses are good places to exercise one's ideals. While campuses may provide academic havens from the community at large, they are still microcosms of society—complete with hierarchical government structures. Beyond prompting gender discussions in the lecture hall and promoting inclusive language, activists on campus might consider the admissions and employment practices of their college or university and the toilet, bathing, and sleeping facilities available to students and faculty. Schools with nondiscrimination policies that include gender identity and expression are more likely to be supportive of gender-variant students and faculty. Some schools have begun providing unisex toilets and bathrooms already. A few offer "gender-blind" housing. In the fall of 2003, Connecticut's Wesleyan University opened a gender-blind floor of dormitory rooms specifically to accommodate gender-variant students. That spring, Smith College, one of the Seven Sisters schools, revised its constitution to omit the word "she" because some of its women students identify as male.[4] (A Smith College student who identifies as male appears in the 2005 Sundance Channel series *TransGeneration*; see the Resources section for more information.) At this point, few campuses have begun to address these issues, providing campus activists with many opportunities to work for change.

To find out how far your school will go to support gender identity and expression, ask to see the school's nondiscrimination policy. To locate other schools' policies, check with the Transgender Law and Policy Institute (TLPI). In August 2004, the TLPI website listed twenty colleges and universities whose nondiscrimination policies include gender identity and expression, and thirty-three (a few of which are included in the first listing) that include such statements in their

GET EQUAL WITH THE ACLU

The American Civil Liberties Union (ACLU) Lesbian and Gay Rights Project has a website called "Get Busy, Get Equal" that provides a nine-step recipe for making your school safe. The steps can be applied to any policy initiative you wish to undertake in your school or community. Following the ACLU directions, from steps about identifying allies and doing policy research at your school, creating your proposal and setting a timeline for your project, to educating others and, finally, presenting your proposal to your school board, you will have a far greater chance of success than if you go it alone. Visit www.aclu.org/getequal/scho/policy2.html and see for yourself.

job listings. When shopping for schools, inquire about the school's dormitory facilities and room assignment policies. Don't assume that schools with coed dorms or bathrooms are sensitive to the needs of androgynous or gender-variant students; ask directly. The more admissions offices field such questions, the sooner schools will seek to accommodate the needs of students whose gender identity or expression does not match their assigned biological sex.

EDUCATE YOUR COMMUNITY

Don't leave the discussions of gender issues to the gender-variant people in your community. Whether you're straight, gay, bisexual, intersex, transgender, queer, or questioning, you have a responsibility to act as an ally for other groups. If you're not present to stand up for the rights of others, how can you expect others to defend your rights should they ever come into question? *Bending the Mold: An Action Kit for Transgender Youth*, published jointly by Lambda Legal and the National Youth Advocacy Coalition (NYAC), is an excellent resource for advocates of transgender teen issues, written specifically for transgender youth. Available from Lambda Legal (see Resources section), the twenty-eight-page booklet includes provocative ideas and gender-bending illustrations to arm yourself for action.

Beyond talking about gender issues, you can make a difference just encouraging others to think about the topic. If

---

SPEAK OUT! WITH HRC
Visit the Human Rights Campaign website at www.hrc.org to find a copy of its twenty-three-page booklet "Speak Out! Activist Tools for GLBT Equality." Filled with practical ideas for how you can make a difference, this guide is indispensable for the developing political activist.

your school does not have a GSA, find individual teachers, counselors, youth ministers, and other adults who would be willing to post "GLBT Safe Zone" stickers, advertising their openness to discussing the issues. Get permission to hang GLBT-friendly notices and posters around campus. Little signs of acceptance can make an enormous difference for someone who is feeling marginalized in his or her community. Everyone likes to be recognized and to see reflections of himself or herself on campus; each person has the right to feel welcome in school and a community. Help make all students feel at home in your school.

Consider waging a campaign at your local library. Befriend a librarian. (They are outstanding people!) Create a wish list of titles you'd like to have available and present it to your local librarian. Ask to have *Gender Identity: The Ultimate Teen Guide* or some of the other resources you have found made available for circulation. Since school and library funds are always tight, consider holding a bake sale or car wash or donating a weekend's wages to accompany your request. If you do, be sure to earmark your donation for gender identity resources and include a list of titles you would like to see added to the library collection.

EXERCISE YOUR POLITICAL VOICE

When you become aware of a legislative issue about which you feel strongly, speak out. If your life feels too busy to allow you to seek out these issues, you can join any number of political action committees (PACs). PACs will keep interested parties aware of the issues important to them through letters or e-mail. Many PACs will send prepared postcards or letters ready to be signed and mailed to legislators; others simply provide key talking points and ask activists to write individual letters. Legislators do listen to what their constituents have to say. An individual handwritten (or typed) letter, into which the writer invested time and thought to write, carries more weight than a cookie-cutter postcard sent in a mass mailing, which required little more than a signature and a stamp. Phone calls, e-mails, faxes, postcards, and letters pour into legislators' offices on a regular basis, and the more effort a sender takes to generate a message, the more weight it will carry in the recipient's office.

If you wish to be politically active without adding your name to PAC mailing lists, visit your local library, read newspapers and magazines, and visit websites found in the Resources section. You can draft correspondence and make phone calls independently of any organization.

Beyond becoming a registered voter and going to the polls on voting days, our political system has room for every citizen's voice; however, only those who speak out are heard. Your opinion matters; make sure your views are heard.

HUMAN RIGHTS CAMPAIGN

Find out about the HRC's Youth College at www.hrc.org/content/navigationmenu/hrc/get_informed/campaigns_and_elections/political_action_committee/hrc_youth_college/hrc_youth_college.htm. The campaign training it offers to twenty energetic people between the ages of eighteen and twenty-four years old during every election cycle is invaluable for current and future political activists.

Some states, including California, Massachusetts, and Washington, have implemented Safe Schools program initiatives. Check the legislative docket in your state to see whether Safe Schools programs are being considered, then be sure to make your legislators aware of your stance on the issue. If the state in which you reside already has a Safe Schools plan in place, find out about it. What is the reporting mechanism? Where should someone direct her or his gender-related Safe Schools concern? How effective is the program? By doing what you can to ensure that any Safe Schools laws in your state are enforced, you can make schools safer for everyone.

MAKE A DIFFERENCE, STARTING TODAY

Today is a good day to begin your campaign to raise awareness of gender-based issues in your school and community. Look around you. Do you see unisex or family restrooms in many places? (Airports are beginning to include family restrooms in order to accommodate all passengers. Although the reason behind their existence may initially have been to accommodate parents traveling with young children, they should also provide safety for persons whose gender expression may be ambiguous.) Take note when completing any application or standard form: must applicants list a gender, and are there only two—male and female—from which to choose? If you are not ready to launch into an educational lecture, simply leave that question blank. Or you might suggest the form provide a blank for gender, which each person can complete in a manner with which they are comfortable. Whenever you encounter a person whose gender appears ambiguous or who otherwise appears

MAKING A DIFFERENCE: BEN A. BARRES

According to Boston Globe staff writer Marcella Bombardieri, Dr. Ben A. Barres, a Stanford University professor of neuroscience, takes exception when he hears sexist remarks about women in the sciences. In fact, in early 2005 when the then president of Harvard University, Lawrence Summers, commented that women don't have the same aptitude for the sciences as do men, Dr. Barres was inspired to act. Before this, Barres had been in denial about gender discrimination in the sciences, despite his own experiences. Until he was in his forties, Barres lived as a female. As a teen, Barbara Barres encountered sexist attitudes as she attempted to pursue study in the sciences. In high school, she was directly discouraged from applying to M.I.T. but did not let that stop her. Undaunted, she pursued her dream and earned degrees from M.I.T., Dartmouth, and Harvard; at the time, she did not feel that being female was an obstacle. Now that Barres has lived as a male for a decade, he has felt the associated privileges. The words for which Summers has since apologized became Barres's catalyst. Thinking back, he could see instances of gender bias that had not previously stopped him. Since then, he has spoken and written about gender bias in the sciences. Bombardieri reports that Barres hopes to continue his feminist activism and to make a difference in the lives of future talented female scientists.[5]

"different" from the norm, do remember to smile or nod hello; this act of welcoming one of society's marginalized citizens is simple enough and may be powerful for the recipient. However you approach the issue, resolve to make a difference in your world—starting today.

NOTES

1. Mireya Navarro, "When Gender Isn't a Given," *New York Times*, Sunday Styles section, 19 September 2004.

2. Janet Lockhart and Susan M. Shaw, *Power of Words: Examining the Language of Ethnic, Gender, and Sexual Orientation Bias*, www.tolerance.org/teach/web/power_of_words/index.jsp; Janet Lockhart and Susan M. Shaw, *Writing for Change: Raising Awareness of Difference, Power, and Discrimination*, www.tolerance.org/teach/web/wfc/index.jsp.

3. www.gsanetwork.org/freezone/aiim/index.html.

4. Jenna Russell, "Finding a Gender-Blind Dorm," *Boston Sunday Globe*, 27 July 2003.

5. Marcella Bombardieri, "Neuroscientist, Once a Woman, Says He Saw Gender Bias Firsthand," *Boston Globe*, 13 July 2006.

Appendix A: Shifting the Paradigm of Intersex Treatment

Alice Dreger, Ph.D.

HELPING PEOPLE UNDER-
STAND GENDER ISSUES
HELPS YOU, TOO

NSSEXUAL

NSGENDER

HAI

Key Points of Comparison	Concealment-Centered Model	Patient-Centered Model
What is intersex?	Intersex is a rare anatomical abnormality which is highly likely to lead to great distress in the family and great distress for the person with an intersex condition. Intersex is pathological and requires immediate medical attention.	Intersex is a relatively common anatomical variation from the "standard" male and female types; just as skin and hair color vary along a wide spectrum, so does sexual and reproductive anatomy. Intersex is neither a medical nor a social pathology.
Is gender determined by nature or nurture?	Nurture. Virtually any child can be made into a "boy" or a "girl" if you just make the genitals look convincing. It doesn't matter what the genes, brain, hormones, and/or prenatal life are/were like.	Both, surely, but that isn't the point. The point is that people with intersex conditions ought to be treated with the same basic ethical principles as everyone else—respect for their autonomy and self-determination, truth about their bodies and their lives, and freedom from discrimination. Physicians, researchers, and gender theorists should stop using people with intersex conditions in "nature/nurture" experiments or debates.

Are intersexed genitals a medical problem?	Yes. Untreated intersex is.	No. Intersexed genitals are not a medical problem. They may signal an underlying metabolic concern, but they themselves are not diseased; they just look different. Metabolic concerns should be treated medically, but intersexed genitals are not in need of medical treatment. There is no evidence for the concealment paradigm, and there is evidence to the contrary.
What should be the medical response?	The correct treatment for intersex is to "normalize" the abnormal genitals using surgical, hormonal, and other technologies. Doing so will eliminate the potential for parents' psychological distress.	The whole family should receive psychosocial support (including referrals to peer support) and as much information as they can handle. True medical problems (like urinary infections and metabolic disorders) should be treated medically, but all nonessential treatments should wait until the person with an intersex condition can consent to them.

(continued)

Key Points of Comparison	Concealment-Centered Model	Patient-Centered Model
When should treatments designed to make a child's genitals look "normal" be done?	As soon as possible, because intersex is a psychosocial emergency. The longer you wait, the greater the trauma.	*Only* if and when the intersexed person requests them, and then only after she or he has been fully informed of the risks and likely outcomes. These surgeries carry substantial risks to life, fertility, continence, and sensation. People with intersex conditions should be able to talk to others who have had the treatments to get their views.
What is motivating this treatment protocol?	The belief that our society can't handle genital ambiguity or nonstandard sexual variation. If we don't fix the genitals, the child with an intersex condition will be ostracized, ridiculed, and rejected, even by his or her own parents.	The belief that the person with an intersex condition has the right to self-determination where her or his body is concerned. Doing "normalizing" surgeries early without the individual's consent interferes with that right; many surgeries and hormone treatments are not reversible. The risks are substantial and should only be taken if the patient has consented.

Question	Answer
Should the parents' distress at their child's condition be treated with surgery on the child?	Yes, absolutely. Parents can and should consent to "normalizing" surgery so that they can fully accept and bond with their child.	Psychological distress is a legitimate concern and should be addressed by properly trained professionals. However, parental distress is not a sufficient reason to risk a child's life, fertility, continence, and sensation.
How do you decide what gender to assign a newborn with an intersex condition?	The doctors decide based on medical tests. If the child has a Y chromosome and an adequate or "reconstructable" penis, the child will be assigned a male gender. (Newborns must have penises of 1 inch or larger if they are to be assigned the male gender.) If the child has a Y chromosome and an inadequate or "unreconstructable" penis according to doctors, the child will be assigned a female gender and surgically	The parents and extended family decide in consultation with the doctors. This approach does not advocate selecting a third or ambiguous gender. The child is assigned a female or male gender, but only after tests (hormonal, genetic, diagnostic) have been done, parents have had a chance to talk with other parents and family members of children with intersex conditions, and the entire family has been

(continued)

Key Points of Comparison	Concealment-Centered Model	Patient-Centered Model
	"reconstructed" as such. If the child has no Y chromosome, it will be assigned the female gender. The genitals will be surgically altered to look more like what doctors think female genitals should look like. This may include clitoral reduction surgeries and construction of a "vagina" (a hole).	offered peer support. We advocate assigning a male or female gender because intersex is not, and will never be, a discrete biological category any more than male or female is, and because assigning an "intersexed" gender would unnecessarily traumatize the child. The doctors and parents recognize, however, that gender assignment of infants with intersex conditions as male or female, as with assignment of any infant, is preliminary. Any child may decide later in life to change their gender assignment; but children with intersex conditions have significantly higher rates of gender transition than the general population, with or without treatment. That is a crucial reason why medically unnecessary surgeries should not be done without the patient's consent; the child with an

Who should counsel the parents when a child with an intersex condition is born?	Intersex is a psychosocial emergency that can be alleviated by quick sex assignment and surgery to reinforce the assignment. Professional counseling is suggested but typically not provided. Peer counseling is typically not suggested or provided.	Intersex is a community and social concern requiring understanding and support. Counseling should begin as soon as the possibility of intersex arises and/or as soon as the family needs it. Professional counselors trained in sex and gender issues, family dynamics, and unexpected birth outcomes should be present. Families should also be actively connected with peer support.
	intersex condition may later want genitals (either the ones they were born with or surgically constructed anatomy) different than what the doctors would have chosen. Surgically constructed genitals are extremely difficult if not impossible to "undo," and children altered at birth or in infancy are largely stuck with what doctors give them.	

(*continued*)

Key Points of Comparison	Concealment-Centered Model	Patient-Centered Model
What should the person with an intersex condition be told when she or he is old enough to understand?	Very little, because telling all we know will just lead to gender confusion that all these surgeries were meant to avoid. Withhold information and records if necessary. Use vague language, like "we removed your twisted ovaries" instead of "we removed your testes" when speaking to a woman with AIS.	Everything known. The person with an intersex condition and parents have the right and responsibility to know as much about intersex conditions as their doctors do. Secrecy and lack of information lead to shame, trauma, and medical procedures that may be dangerous to the patient's health. Conversely, some people harmed by secrecy and shame may avoid future health care. For example, women with AIS may avoid medical care, including needed hormone replacement therapy.
What's wrong with the opposing paradigm?	Parents and peers might be uncomfortable with a child with ambiguous genitalia. Social institutions and settings like locker rooms, public restrooms, daycare centers, and schools will be brutal environments for an "abnormal" child. The person with	The autonomy and right to self-determination of the person with an intersex condition is violated by the surgery-centered model. In the concealment model, surgeries are done without truly obtaining consent; parents

	an intersex condition might later wish that her or his parents had chosen to have her or his genitals "normalized."	are often not told the failure rate of, lack of evidentiary support for, and alternatives to surgery. Social distress is a reason to change society, not the bodies of children.
What is the ideal future of intersex?	Elimination via improved scientific and medical technologies.	Social acceptance of human diversity and an end to the idea that difference equals disease.
Who are the proponents of each paradigm?	John Money and his followers, most pediatric urologists and pediatric endocrinologists, and many gynecologists and other health care practitioners.	Intersex activists and their supporters, ethicists, some legal scholars, medical historians, and a growing number of clinicians.

Prepared by Alice Dreger, Ph.D., for the Intersex Society of North America, 15 July 2004. For additional reading or to download a copy of this protocol, please visit the website of the Intersex Society of North America, www.isna.org.

Appendix B:
A Bill of
Gender Rights

JoAnn Roberts, Ph.D.

HELPING PEOPLE UNDER-
STAND GENDER ISSUES
HELPS YOU, TOO

It is time for the transgendered community to take a stand, a strong stand, against all gender-based discrimination simply because some people are different and simply because some people do not fit into current social norms of gender roles. It is time the gender-based community articulate this stand in words that clearly define exactly what our gender rights are. It is time to stand alongside other minority rights movements to declare these gender rights as follows:

THE RIGHT TO ASSUME A GENDER ROLE

Every human being has within themselves an idea of who they are and what they are capable of achieving. That identity and capability shall not be limited by a person's physical or genetic sex, nor by what any society may deem as "masculine" or "feminine" behavior. It is fundamental, then, that each individual has the right to assume gender roles congruent with one's self-perceived identity and capabilities, regardless of physical sex, genetic sex, or sex role. Therefore, no person shall be denied their Human and/or Civil Rights on the basis that their gender role or perceived gender role is not congruent with their genetic sex, physical sex, or sex role.

THE RIGHT TO FREELY EXPRESS GENDER ROLES

Given that each individual has the right to assume gender roles, it then follows that each individual has the right to freely

165

express gender roles in any manner that does not infringe on the freedom of another individual. Therefore, no person shall be denied their Human and/or Civil Rights on the basis that a private or public expression of a gender role or perceived gender role is not congruent with their physical sex, genetic sex, or sex role.

THE RIGHT TO MAKE ONE'S BODY CONGRUENT WITH GENDER ROLE

Given that each individual has the right to assume gender roles, it then follows that each individual has the right to change their body or alter its physiology so it better fits a gender role. These changes may be cosmetically, chemically, or surgically induced, provided these changes are supervised by an appropriate licensed professional and the individual accepts sole responsibility for their actions in this regard. Therefore, no person shall be denied their Human and/or Civil Rights on the basis that they changed or wish to change their body, cosmetically, chemically, surgically, or any combination of these, to better fit a gender role.

THE RIGHT TO SEXUAL EXPRESSION CONGRUENT WITH GENDER ROLE

Given that each individual has the right to assume gender roles, it then follows that each individual has the right to express their sexuality within a gender role. Therefore, no person shall be denied their Human and/or Civil Rights on the basis of sexual orientation or perceived sexual orientation. Further, no individual shall be denied their Human and/or Civil Rights for expressing a gender role through private sexual acts between consenting adults in any manner that does not infringe on the freedom of another individual.

JoAnn Roberts, Ph.D., December 1990 © 1999 by cdspub.com and 3-D Com., Inc.

JoAnn Roberts is one of the cofounders of the Renaissance Transgender Education Association and has served on the boards of most major transgender organizations. She is a publisher and journalist. As an activist in the 1990s she penned the Gender Bill of Rights in December 1990 as a focal point for transgender political action. Roberts, along with Phyllis Randolph Frye (founder of International Conference of Transgender Law and Employment Policy) and Kymberleigh Richards (publisher of *Cross-Talk* magazine) popularized the use of "transgender" to encompass all gender-different people.

Resources

HELPING PEOPLE UNDER-
STAND GENDER ISSUES
HELPS YOU, TOO

This book is meant to provide an introductory overview of gender identity issues for any inquiring mind. To learn more, venture beyond the covers of this book. Living in the information age affords us advantages such as a wealth of resources providing information and support in various media. Here is a list to get you started; it is by no means exhaustive. Each source has the potential for providing you with other sources.

ORGANIZATIONS

Gender-Related

American Educational Gender Information Service, Inc. (AEGIS)
P.O. Box 33724
Decatur, GA 30033
aegis@mindspring.com
www.gender.org/aegis

Founded in 1990, AEGIS prides itself on providing commonsense quality information for transgendered and transsexual persons. A nonprofit organization since 1994, AEGIS members receive *Chrysalis* magazine, *AEGIS News*, and other materials. Although AEGIS was succeeded by Gender Education and Advocacy (GEA) in 1998, it still exists as a project of GEA.

Gender Education and Advocacy (GEA)
P.O. Box 33724
Decatur, GA 30033
www.gender.org

GEA is a nonprofit corporation and the successor organization to AEGIS, which operated independently between 1990 and 1998. GEA provides free information about gender variance and encourages the distribution of its material for educational purposes.

Gender Education Center (GEC)
P.O. Box 1861
Maple Grove, MN 55311
Tel: (763) 424-5445
www.debradavis.org
GEC is an advocacy and educational nonprofit organization working toward understanding, acceptance, and support for the GLBT community with an emphasis on differently gendered people. Started in 1990, GEC became a Minnesota-based nonprofit in 1994.

Harry Benjamin International Gender
    Dysphoria Association (HBIGDA)
1300 South Second Street, Suite 180
Minneapolis, MN 55454
Tel: (612) 624-9397
hbigda@umphysicians.umn.edu
www.hbigda.org
HBIGDA, a professional organization devoted to the understanding and treatment of gender identity disorders, develops and promotes the internationally accepted HBIGDA Standards of Care, first published in 1979, for the treatment of gender identity disorders. Its website provides links for professionals to transgender organizations and information, gender programs and service centers, and sexology organizations and information resources.

International Foundation for Gender Education (IFGE)
P.O. Box 540229
Waltham, Mass. 02454
Tel: (781) 899-2212
www.ifge.org

IFGE is a nonprofit membership organization, founded in 1987, that provides information, education, and other resources to the trans community, their family and friends, educators, and other professionals. IFGE publishes *Transgender Tapestry* magazine and *Thread* newsletter, maintains the Synchronicity Bookstore and the Winslow Street Fund, offers TSELF scholarships, and sponsors an annual conference on sex and gender.

Intersex Society of North America (ISNA)
Cheryl Chase, Executive Director
4500 9th Avenue, N.E., #300
Seattle, WA 98105
979 Golf Course Drive, #282
Rohnert Park, CA 94928
www.isna.org
ISNA, founded in 1993, works to improve the social and medical treatment received by persons with intersex conditions through educating medical practitioners and the public at large about the concerns of intersex persons.

Parents, Families, and Friends of Lesbians and Gays (PFLAG)
1726 M Street, NW, Suite 400
Washington, DC 20036
Tel: (202) 467-8180
www.pflag.org
PFLAG (pronounced "P-flag") was formally started in 1973 by the parents of a gay man who saw—on television—their son being attacked at a gay rights demonstration and the failure of police to intervene. PFLAG became a national organization in 1981. Now a major nonprofit organization with more than 500 United States affiliates, PFLAG, the parents, families, and friends of lesbian, gay, bisexual, and transgendered persons, celebrates diversity and envisions a world where all people are respected. Transgender-specific resources can be located at the home site for PFLAG's TransGender Support (TGS-PFLAG) List-serv; refer to the Internet Resources portion of this Resource listing for information.

Sexuality Information and Education Council
    of the United States (SIECUS)
130 West 42nd Street, Suite 350
New York, NY 10036
Tel: (212) 819-9770
www.siecus.org

   Incorporated in 1964, SIECUS is a national nonprofit organization that affirms that sexuality is a natural and healthy part of living. A superb clearinghouse for information about sexuality, their Families Are Talking website (www.familiesaretalking.org) provides a wealth of information to promote family conversations about sexuality and sex education.

Legal and Political

American Civil Liberties Union
125 Broad Street, 18th Floor
New York, NY 10004
www.aclu.org

   The ACLU's main focus is defending the Bill of Rights. Founded in 1920, this nonprofit organization actively defends student rights in several areas, and the Youth & Schools arm of its Lesbian and Gay Rights subdivision aims to make schools safe for LGBT youth.

Gay & Lesbian Advocates & Defenders (GLAD)
30 Winter Street, Suite 800
Boston, MA 02108
Tel: (617) 426-1350
www.glad.org

   Founded in 1978, GLAD is New England's leading civil rights organization dedicated to ending discrimination based on sexual orientation, HIV status, and gender identity and expression. This is the nonprofit organization that filed and won the "freedom to marry" case in Massachusetts.

Gay & Lesbian Alliance Against Defamation (GLAAD)
5455 Wilshire Blvd., #1500

Los Angeles, CA 90036
Tel: (323) 933-2240
www.glaad.org
   Formed in 1985, GLAAD works to promote fair, accurate, and inclusive representation of people and events in the media as a means of eliminating homophobia and discrimination based on gender identity and sexual orientation.

Human Rights Campaign (HRC)
1640 Rhode Island Avenue, NW
Washington, DC 20036
www.hrc.org
   Established in 1980, the HRC provides a national voice on gay and lesbian issues. HRC actively works for lesbian, gay, bisexual, and transgender equal rights through the political arena and organizes and educates at the grassroots level. Through its Youth College for Campaign Training program, HRC recruits, trains, and employs future political activists each election cycle.

Lambda Legal
120 Wall Street, Suite 1500
New York, NY 10005
Tel: (212) 809-8585
www.lambdalegal.org
   Lambda Legal (previously known as the Lambda Legal Defense and Education Fund) is a national organization committed to achieving full recognition of the civil rights of lesbians, gay men, bisexuals, the transgendered, and people with HIV or AIDS, through impact litigation, education, and public policy work. Formed in 1973 after the New York Supreme Court overturned a ruling that had denied its application to become a nonprofit organization, Lambda Legal has served as a leader in securing LGBT rights for more than thirty years.

National Gay and Lesbian Task Force (NGLTF)
1325 Massachusetts Avenue, NW, Suite 600
Washington, DC 20005
Tel: (202) 393-5177
www.thetaskforce.org

Founded in 1973, NGLTF is a national organization seeking civil rights for LGBT people. It hosts an annual Creating Change conference.

National Transgender Advocacy Coalition (NTAC)
P.O. Box 76027
Washington, DC 20013
www.ntac.org

NTAC is a nonprofit activist organization that works for the advancement of understanding and the attainment of full civil rights for all transgendered, intersex, and gender-variant people in every aspect of society. Founded in 1999, NTAC is a federal-level lobbyist, a supporter of state-level lobbying, and a nonprofit corporation.

Southern Poverty Law Center (SPLC)
400 Washington Avenue
Montgomery, AL 36104
Tel: (334) 956-8200
www.tolerance.org

Dedicated to fighting hate and promoting tolerance, the SPLC is a national nonprofit organization. Founded in 1971 as a small civil rights law firm, it is now respected for its many programs and projects. Teaching Tolerance is a program that provides free curriculum materials to teachers. Mix It Up is a project geared to student activists. The center's website, Tolerance.org, provides free downloadable public service announcements and more.

Youth-Oriented

Boston Alliance of Gay, Lesbian, Bisexual,
   and Transgender Youth (BAGLY)
35 Bowdoin Street
Boston, MA 02114
Tel: (617) 227-4313
TTY: (617) 523-8341
www.bagly.org

In operation since 1980 and well-respected in the community, BAGLY is dedicated to creating safe space where youth are free to explore their identities. Youth-led and adult-supported, it serves GLBTQQ and allied youth age 22 and under. BAGLY offers weekly gatherings, unprecedented social events (including the LGBT prom, which now draws 1,500 attendees annually), plus resources and referrals. BAGLY's Queer Activist College offers antihomophobia and antiracism training and facilitates public-speaking and leadership skills.

Children of Lesbians and Gays Everywhere (COLAGE)
1550 Bryant Street, Suite 830
San Francisco, CA 94103
Tel: (415) 861-KIDS
www.colage.org
    An outgrowth of Just for Us conferences in the late 1980s, COLAGE adopted its present name in 1993. COLAGE is the only national and international organization designed to support youth with gay, lesbian, bisexual, and transgender parents. COLAGE chapters are self-run groups operating in North America, Sweden, and England so far. Find a group in your area, or start one!

Gay–Straight Alliance (GSA) Network
160 14th Street
San Francisco, CA 94103
www.gsanetwork.org
    The GSA Network links GSAs in California and provides a wealth of information for anyone interested in creating a GSA.

Lavender Youth Recreation and Information Center (LYRIC)
127 Collingwood Street
San Francisco, CA 94114
Tel: (415) 703-6150
Youth Hotline: 800-96-YOUTH (outside California) or 800-246-PRIDE (within California)
www.lyric.org
    LYRIC is a community center for lesbian, gay, bisexual, transgender, queer, and questioning youth age 23 and under. Its

Asian Pacific Islander (API) Family Project offers support to LGBTQQ youth and families of API heritage, whose culture and traditions differ from the Western norm. Online, LYRIC offers links to a variety of informational resources.

National Youth Advocacy Coalition (NYAC)
1638 R Street, NW, Suite 300
Washington, DC 20009
Tel: (800) 541-6922
www.nyacyouth.org

Founded in 1993, NYAC is a social justice organization advocating for and with lesbian, gay, bisexual, transgender, and questioning youth to end discrimination against these individuals and to ensure their well-being. Their website provides extensive social, political, and health-related information.

Project 10
www.project10.org

Dr. Virginia Uribe,
    Executive Director
Friends of Project 10
115 W. California Boulevard #116
Pasadena, CA 91105
Tel: (626) 577-4553
project10@hotmail.com

Gail Rolf,
    Project 10 Adviser
Los Angeles Unified
    School District
355 South Grand Avenue,
    KPMG, 10th Floor
Los Angeles, CA 90071
Tel: (213) 633-7826
grolf@lausd.k12.ca.us

Founded in 1984 by Dr. Virginia Uribe, a former high school teacher, Project 10 provides educational support services to LGBTQ students who attend public schools in the Los Angeles Unified School District. Portions of the Project 10 model are replicated in schools across the country (e.g., Project 10 East in Cambridge, Massachusetts).

Syndrome-Related

Androgen Insensitivity Syndrome Support Group (AISSG)–USA
P.O. Box 2148

Duncan, OK 73534
www.medhelp.org/ais

Hypospadias & Epispadias Association (HEA)
P.O. Box 1422
Somerset, TX 78069
www.heainfo.org

Klinefelter Syndrome and Associates (KS&A)
11 Keats Court
Coto de Caza, CA 92679
http://genetic.org/ks
Toll Free: (888) 999-9428

Mayer-Rotikansky-Kuster-Hauser Syndrome Organization
(MRKH.org)
P.O. Box 301494
Jamaica Plain, MA 02130
www.MRKH.org
info@mrkh.org

Turner Syndrome Society (TSS)–United States
14450 TC Jester, Suite 260
Houston, TX 77014
Toll Free: (800) 365-9944
www.turner-syndrome-us.org

INTERNET RESOURCES

Beyond the websites listed for the organizations above, the following additional Internet resources are available.

The Freedom to Marry Coalition of Massachusetts
www.equalmarriage.org
A political group active in supporting same-sex marriage rights.

Gender Talk
www.gendertalk.com

The website for Gender Talk radio offers trans-relevant information, audio clips, pertinent links, and more than 400 archived programs dating back to 1997 available for download.

Kael's Page
http://kpscapes.tripod.com
One person's continuing journey in search of self. Kael, a twenty-something female-to-male transsexual, keeps a record of his journey across genders on this user-friendly, award-winning website. Extensive information, links, and resources.

MassEquality.Org
www.massequality.org
MassEquality.Org supports marriage rights for everyone regardless of gender.

Oasis Magazine
www.oasismag.com
A creative writing community for GLBTQQ youth that includes essays, artwork, poetry, and online journals.

The P.E.R.S.O.N. Project
www.personproject.org
Extensive news, legal, and educational resources for K–12 educators, GLBT youth, and their allies. Offers an invaluable organizing handbook with state-by-state legal information for those interested in "organizing for educational equity." The website's numerous awards date back to 1997.

QueerTheory.com
www.queertheory.com
An online resource for visual and textual resources in queer culture, queer theory, queer studies, gender studies, and related fields.

TGWorld
www.tgworld.org

TGWorld describes itself as providing a safe place for the transgender community to live and learn. TGWorld includes links to information and articles; a worldwide list of TGWorld organizations by country, with organizations listed in 46 states of the United States; mail list discussions for the transgender public, transgender members, and transgender veterans; a personal page; and the TGWorld webring of transgender community sites. TGWorld is funded by sponsor links and the individual donations of visitors.

Tolerance.org
www.tolerance.org/teens
Built to "fight hate and promote tolerance," this website of the Southern Poverty Law Center hosts "Mix It Up" and provides an excellent resource site for teen activists. See also *Teaching Tolerance* magazine, no. 27 (Spring 2005), which includes articles, activities, and curriculum guides relating to gender, identity, and language.

TransGender Care
www.transgendercare.com
A comprehensive educational resource begun by Dr. Carl Bushong in 1977 as an outgrowth of the Tampa Stress Center. Provides answers to basic questions, material for research papers, and specialized information for transgender, transsexual, transvestite, and cross-dressing persons.

Transgender Law & Policy Institute (TLPI)
www.transgenderlaw.org
TLPI is a nonprofit organization dedicated to effective advocacy for transgender people. Find up-to-date listings about nondiscrimination laws and policies as they pertain to gender identity/expression, including listings of colleges and universities whose policies include such statements and/or who may not discriminate due to nondiscrimination laws affecting them.

TransGender Services–Parents, Families and Friends
    of Lesbians and Gays (TGS-PFLAG)
www.critpath.org/pflag-talk/tgsfaq.html

PFLAG supports parents, families, and friends of transgender persons through TGS-PFLAG. Monitored discussion is open to TGS-PFLAG List-serv members. A wealth of resources, including lists for specific subsections of the transgender community and transgender-specific PFLAG groups are available here.

TransProud
www.transproud.com
TransProud, OutProud's World Wide Website for transgender youth, includes a welcome page for parents newly learning about transgender issues (http://www.transproud .com/parents.html), as well as links to QueerAmerica transgender resource listings and to Outpath personal narratives by transgender youth.

Trans Youth WebRing
http://dir.webring.com/hub?ring=transyouth
Some excellent links for trans teens, including sites by trans youth, can be found here. Beware of any links to nude models and porn stars. Links to regional groups, personal sites of various trans youth, and more.

Youth Resource: A Project of Advocates for Youth
www.youthresource.com
Created for GLBTQ youth ages 13 to 24, this user-friendly site offers a wealth of information and links. Taking a holistic approach to sexual health and well-being, Youth Resource provides support, resources, community, and peer-to-peer education.

MOVIES

The Birdcage. Directed by Mike Nichols. 119 min. MGM Home Entertainment, 1996. Rated R.
A comedy wherein a young man's liberal gay fathers masquerade as a heterosexual couple one evening in order to

meet the conservative heterosexual parents of the man's fiancée. While one father presents as a woman, the other works to be perceived as wholly masculine. A campy remake of the classic French farce *La Cage aux Folles* (1978).

Boys Don't Cry. Directed by Kimberly Pierce. 118 min. Twentieth Century Fox, 1999. Rated R.

A compelling drama based upon the life of Brandon Teena, a female-to-male transsexual who was brutally murdered when her gender was discovered.

Call Me Malcolm. Produced by Joseph Parlagreco and Kierra Chase. 90 min. Filmworks and the United Church of Christ, 2004. Unrated.

A moving, feature-length documentary about a twenty-seven-year-old transgender seminary student and his struggle with faith, love, and gender identity.

The Crying Game. Directed by Neil Jordan. 112 min. Miramax Films, 1992. Rated R.

A psychological thriller wherein an Irish Republican Army soldier tracks down the girlfriend of a former IRA hostage and falls for her, then learns she has male anatomy.

A Girl Like Me: The Gwen Araujo Story. Directed by Agnieszka Holland. Braun Entertainment/Sony Pictures, 2006. Unrated.

This Lifetime Original feature-length movie depicts the true story of Gwen Araujo, a transgender teen who was brutally murdered in San Francisco.

Ma Vie En Rose. Directed by Alain Berliner. 88 min. Sony Pictures Classics/Columbia Tristar Home, 1997. Rated R.

A sensitive drama following the life of a young boy who feels like a girl. In French with English subtitles.

Mrs. Doubtfire. Directed by Chris Columbus. 125 min. 20th Century Fox Home Entertainment, 1993. Rated PG-13.

A lighthearted comedy about a divorced man so desperate to see his children that he poses for the job of his ex-wife's housekeeper and becomes a nanny to his children.

Normal. Directed by Jane Anderson. 110 min. HBO Films, 2003. Unrated.

A made-for-cable film documenting the transition of a male-to-female transsexual in a small midwestern town who comes out about feeling trapped in a man's body after twenty-five successful years of marriage.

Soldier's Girl. Directed by Frank Pierson. 112 min. Showtime Entertainment, 2003. Rated R.

A docudrama set in Tennessee about a group of soldiers who become violent toward a fellow soldier when they learn he's dating a transsexual performer.

That's a Family! Directed by Debra Chasnoff. 35 min. Women's Educational Media, 2000. Unrated.

Geared toward K–8 audiences but effective with groups of all ages, this brief documentary film is an excursion into the composition of today's American families. In it, children speak candidly about their family experiences, and provide many entrance points for discussion.

Tootsie. Directed by Sydney Pollack. 116 min. Columbia Tristar Home Video, 1982. Rated PG.

A comedy about an underemployed male actor who applies for a female role on a television soap opera, succeeds, then falls for a woman and is courted by an older man.

TransAmerica. Directed by Duncan Tucker. 103 min. IFC Films and the Weinstein Company, 2005. Rated R.

A comedic drama about a male-to-female transsexual who, while saving to pay for sexual reassignment surgery, is contacted by a son—the product of a long-ago sexual liaison when she was a man—with whom she undertakes a cross-country trek, without first identifying herself as the young man's father.

Victor/Victoria. Directed by Blake Edwards. 146 min. Image Entertainment/Metropolitan Entertainment, 1982. Rated PG-13.

An entertaining comedy about a woman pretending to be a man impersonating a woman.

Wilde. Directed by Brian Gilbert. 116 min. Samuelson Entertainment, 1998. Rated R.

A docudrama about the tragic life of nineteenth-century British writer Oscar Wilde, who discovers homosexual love and its legal consequences while a husband and a father.

The World According to Garp. Directed by George Roy Hill. 137 min. Warner Brothers, 1982. Rated R.

A comic drama based on the novel by John Irving. T. S. Garp grows up at a boarding school for boys where his mother works as the nurse; becomes a writer, a husband, and a father; and follows his mother's career as she chooses to work with sexually damaged persons at a private seaside resort. A prominent character is a caring male-to-female transsexual who was formerly a professional football player.

RADIO

Gender Talk radio, in the Greater Boston area, airs on WMBR 88.1 FM every Saturday evening 8:00–9:00 P.M. Eastern time. Or, visit the website (www.gendertalk.com or http://wmbr.org) to listen to current or archived shows any time. Gender Talk radio bills itself as "the leading worldwide weekly radio program that talks about transgenderism in the first person."

TransFM, the Transgender Comedy Show, is just one of several transgender shows broadcast via Live365 Radio, which can be listened to at www.transfm.org. The comedy show contains "adult humor and issues" and is intended for mature audiences only.

TELEVISION AND CABLE

Check the listings for the Discovery Channel, the Discovery Health Channel, the Learning Channel, A&E, and PBS periodically for relevant programming. Broadcasts focused on gender issues occur from time to time, all with an educational focus, with new shows generated each year. A few of those developed for broadcast in the last few years are listed below.

"Gender: Unknown." Discovery Health Channel, 2000.
　　Examines the lives and gender experiences of three intersex persons who, at one time, might have worked as circus side show freaks.

Role Reversal. A&E Television Network, 2002.
　　Follows four adults—two male and two female—through a month in New York City as they experiment with living as the opposite sex. Extensive counseling and coaching are provided as the subjects attempt to transform themselves physically, mentally, and emotionally.

"Sex: Unknown." *NOVA.* PBS, 30 October 2001.
　　Explores the case of David Reimer, "the boy who was raised as a girl," and corresponding medical research of the time.

Taboo. National Geographic Channel.
　　The episode "Sexuality" first aired in 2002, while "Gender Benders" aired in 2004.

"Transgender Revolution." *The Point.* A&E Television Network, 2002.
　　Explores gender oppression, interviewing transsexuals, a neurosurgical specialist, and a Gender PAC lobbyist.

"Transgender Teens." Discovery Health Channel, 2003.

Examines the lives of two transgendered male-to-female teens, both with very different experiences—one who has family support and one who survives on the streets.

"TransGeneration." Sundance Channel, 20 September 2005.
An original documentary, following four transitioning transgender college students through an undergraduate year as they live out and proud on campus.

BOOKS AND PAMPHLETS

Nonfiction and Curriculum Materials

Baird, Vanessa. *The No-Nonsense Guide to Sexual Diversity*. Toronto: New Internationalist Publications and Between the Lines, 2001.
Part of the New Internationalist and Between the Lines's growing No-Nonsense Guide series, this pocket-sized title addresses sexual diversity around the globe.

Boenke, Mary, ed. *Trans Forming Families: Real Stories about Transgendered Loved Ones*. 2nd ed. New Castle, Del.: Oak Knoll Press, 2003.
Edited by the parent of a female-to-male transgendered son, this family-oriented book is written for families and friends who wish to understand transgendered persons. Educational and comprehensive, it includes personal stories of acceptance of transgendered persons.

Califia, Patrick. *Sex Changes: The Politics of Transgenderism*. 2nd ed. San Francisco: Cleis Press, 2003.
This direct and explicit exploration of the psychology, sociology, and politics of sexuality, challenging the male/female norm, is written by an outspoken sex radical and therapist.

Feinberg, Leslie. *Transgender Warriors: Making History from Joan of Arc to Dennis Rodman*. Boston: Beacon Press, 1996.

A comprehensive overview of trans people in history. Feinberg ensures that his readers are aware of the depth and breadth of trans people's experiences in our world.

———. *Trans Liberation: Beyond Pink or Blue*. Boston: Beacon Press, 1998.
A collection of Feinberg's passionate speeches in favor of an equitable society for all genders.

Garner, Abigail. *Families Like Mine: Children of Gay Parents Tell It Like It Is*. New York: HarperCollins, 2004.
Based upon personal experience, as well as interviews with fifty grown children of gay, lesbian, bisexual, or transgender parents, Garner's book effectively contradicts the myths about children of gay parents growing up "damaged" because of the parents. Instead, the author cites the stresses of daily living in a homophobic society as children of gay parents. Recommended for gay parents and parents-to-be, families of gay parents, and friends of children with gay parents.

Gay–Straight Alliance Network. *Take It Back: A Manual for Fighting Slurs on Campus*. San Francisco: Tides Center/Gay-Straight Alliance Network, 2003.
This comprehensive manual for teen activists is available free online for those interested in combating the power of hurtful words.

Gerdes, R. Scott, and Debra Davis, "I Think I Might Be Transgender . . . Now What Do I Do?" Maple Grove, Minn.: Gender Education Center, 1999.
This pamphlet offers supportive information written for questioning teen readers by a transgender writer and an out transgender high school librarian. Visit the Gender Education Center's award-winning website to find it.

Howard, Kim, and Annie Stevens. *Out and About Campus: Personal Accounts by Lesbian, Gay, Bisexual, and Transgendered College Students*. Los Angeles: Alyson, 2000.

This collection of personal stories from twenty-eight college students on campuses across the United States provides current and prospective students, their families, allies, faculty, and staff with a sense of what college life has been for these individuals.

Huegel, Kelly. *GLBTQ (Gay, Lesbian, Bisexual, Transgender, and Questioning): The Survival Guide for Queer and Questioning Teens*. Minneapolis, Minn.: Free Spirit, 2003.
   A must-read for queer and questioning teens and the people who care about them, *GLBTQ* is chock-full of facts, resources, and sound advice.

Hunter, Nan D., Courtney G. Joslin, and Sharon M. McGowan. *The Rights of Lesbians, Gay Men, Bisexuals, and Transgender People: The Authoritative Guide to a Lesbian, Gay, Bisexual, or Transgender Person's Rights*. 4th ed. Carbondale: Southern Illinois University Press, 2004.
   Originally published in 1975, this ACLU handbook has been updated again. This fourth edition includes contact information for legal groups across the nation and a summary describing individual state laws.

Jennings, Kevin, with Pat Shapiro. *Always My Child: A Parent's Guide to Understanding Your Gay, Lesbian, Bisexual, Transgendered, or Questioning Son or Daughter*. New York: Simon & Schuster/Fireside, 2003.
   Written especially for parents, this book emphasizes the need for families to make the home a haven. Using personal experience, true stories, and scientific research, Jennings advises parents on how to become familiar with their child's culture and how to watch for signs of distress.

Lambda Legal and the National Youth Advocacy Coalition. "Bending the Mold: An Action Kit for Transgender Youth." N.p.: Lambda Legal Defense and Education Foundation and National Youth Advocacy Coalition, 2004.
   Written specifically for transgender youth, this downloadable pamphlet is designed to help young trans people navigate their world successfully and proudly.

Lockhart, Janet, and Susan M. Shaw. *The Power of Words: Examining the Language of Ethnic, Gender, and Sexual Orientation Bias*. Montgomery, Ala.: Teaching Tolerance, 2005.

Written for educators and group leaders, this curriculum unit provides lesson plans, reproducible handouts, and other resources for considering the impact of biased words in our world.

Moir, Anne, and David Jessel. *Brain Sex: The Real Difference between Men and Women*. New York: Dell, 1992.

Although its content is controversial, this book provides fascinating reading for anyone interested in how brains vary by gender.

Moulton, Brian, and Liz Seaton. *Transgender Americans: A Handbook for Understanding*. Washington, D.C.: Human Rights Campaign, 2005.

A comprehensive handbook about transgender issues, covering topics from discrimination to marriage and family, *Transgender Americans* is available free for download at www.hrc.org.

Rose, Lannie. *How to Change Your Sex: A Lighthearted Look at the Hardest Thing You'll Ever Do*. Raleigh, N.C.: Lulu Enterprises, 2004.

Written by an author who did not recognize that she was transsexual until the age of forty-six and who is now living as a woman, this "how to" book is written for anyone with gender issues and the families, friends, and helping professionals in his or her life.

Rudacille, Deborah. *The Riddle of Gender: Science, Activism, and Transgender Rights*. New York: Pantheon Books, 2005.

A comprehensive overview of past and current thinking about gender issues, written by a science writer with no previous involvement with transgender issues. This book makes the issues approachable and gives readers intriguing glimpses into transgender experience.

Sember, Brett McWhorter. *Gay and Lesbian Rights: A Guide for GLBT Singles, Couples and Families*. Naperville, Ill.: Sphinx, 2003.

 This user-friendly guide includes much solid information and many resources for LGBT persons and allies. (The Rights series by Sphinx Publishing also includes *Teen Rights* by Traci Truly.)

Biographies and Memoirs

Boylan, Jennifer Finney. *She's Not There: A Life in Two Genders*. New York: Random House/Broadway Books, 2003.

 The memoir of a male-to-female transsexual. James Finney Boylan became Jennifer Finney Boylan at forty-four, when she was a successful husband and father of two, and a novelist chairing the English Department at Colby College in Maine. Her life has continued to be much the same as before since the gender-reassignment surgery.

Brevard, Aleshia. *The Woman I Was Not Born to Be: A Transsexual Journey*. Philadelphia: Temple University Press, 2001.

 The autobiography of a male-to-female transsexual, born Alfred Brevard Crenshaw in 1937 Tennessee, who had transsexual surgery in the 1960s and became a successful entertainer, Playboy bunny, and B-movie starlet.

Colapinto, John. *As Nature Made Him: The Boy Who Was Raised as a Girl*. New York: HarperCollins, 2000.

 The biography of David Reimer, "the boy who was raised as a girl" from age two through fourteen.

Howey, Noelle. *Dress Codes: Of Three Girlhoods, My Mother's, My Father's, and Mine*. New York: Picador USA, 2002.

 This memoir offers a daughter's coming-of-age recollections, her parents' stories, and Noelle's experience of her father choosing to live as a woman.

Jorgensen, Christine, with Susan Stryker. *Christine Jorgensen: A Personal Autobiography*. 2nd ed. San Francisco: Cleis Press, 2000.

Written by an ex-GI who traveled to Sweden for a much-publicized sex change operation in 1952, Jorgensen's story brought international media attention to transsexual surgery and provided inspiration to countless gender-variant persons by setting a proud example.

Lady Chablis, with Theodore Bouloukos. *Hiding My Candy*. New York: Pocket Books, 1996.

The autobiography of a self-proclaimed woman who is anatomically male (although hormones have enhanced her breasts and caused [his] impotence). The story of a survivor with a devilish sense of humor.

Lees, Lisa. *Fragments of Gender*. East Lansing, Mich.: Phreeky Dragon Press, 2005.

A collection of poetry, stories, and personal essays compiled by a transgender woman over the first ten years after her transition and published via Lulu.com.

Middlebrook, Diane Wood. *Suits Me: The Double Life of Billy Tipton*. Boston: Houghton-Mifflin, 1998.

A successful jazzman is discovered to be female upon his death.

O'Keefe, Tracie, and Katrina Fox. *Finding the Real Me: True Tales of Sex and Gender Diversity*.

A collection of first-person narratives by more than two dozen sex- and gender-diverse adults from around the globe, about their own experiences with sex and gender.

Trope, Zoe. *Please Don't Kill the Freshman: A Memoir*. New York: HarperCollins, 2003.

Written by a high school student experiencing the highs and lows of her sophomore year, this insightful, sometimes cryptic journal includes flashes of beauty and moments of despair. Zoe struggles with being a teenager, understanding her own gender and sexuality and those of her friends, managing notoriety and book contracts, and the confusion of being a girl who has a girlfriend when Zoe does not identify as a lesbian, then having that girlfriend become a "boifriend."

Fiction

Bauer, Marion Dane. *Am I Blue? Coming Out from the Silence.* New York: HarperCollins, 1994.

This collection of short stories by prominent young adult authors deals with gay issues for teens. The title story, "Am I Blue?" by Bruce Coville, is a satirical fairy tale wherein a male fairy comes to the rescue of a boy who is being harassed because his peers perceive him to be gay. Caustic yet funny, Coville uses stereotypes to educate without preaching.

Bohjalian, Chris. *Trans-Sister Radio.* New York: Harmony Books, 2000. Paperback, New York: Vintage Contemporaries, 2001.

A sleepy little Vermont town hosts this tale of a MTF transsexual through her transition. Four narrators and public radio broadcast transcripts provide multiple points of view.

Eugenidies, Jeffrey. *Middlesex.* New York: Farrar, Straus and Giroux, 2002.

An intergenerational Greek American family saga spanning continents, this best-selling, award-winning novel is ultimately the story of Cal Stephanides, who was born and raised as Calliope until, as a teenager, he was discovered to be a hermaphrodite.

Feinberg, Leslie. *Stone Butch Blues.* Los Angeles: Alyson Books, 2003.

Set in upper New York State in the years surrounding the Stonewall Rebellion, this is a historically accurate coming-of-age story of a butch lesbian who eventually makes the FTM transition and lives as a man.

Hall, Radclyffe. *The Well of Loneliness*. New York: Doubleday, 1928.

Set in turn-of-the-twentieth-century Europe, where neither homosexuality nor gender dysphoria were accepted or understood, Hall's autobiographical novel was banned in Britain upon publication for its lesbian content and allowed into the United States only after an extended court battle. An early work focused on gender dysphoria, this now-classic lesbian love story is a study in how society teaches those who are different to hate themselves for that difference.

Lees, Lisa. *Fool for Love*. East Lansing, Mich.: Phreeky Dragon Press, 2005.

Written by a transsexual woman to fit a gap she perceived on the shelves of young-adult fiction, *Fool for Love* tells the story of Carys and Jamie, two girls who don't fit the expectations for their gender. Carys has never worn a dress and Jamie is intersex. When they fall in love, both begin a journey of self-discovery and, ultimately, trust.

Matthews, Andrew. *The Flip Side*. New York: Delacorte Press, 2003.

In a book set in present-day Crossleigh, England, fifteen-year-old Robert Hunt must wear a dress to play Rosalind in Shakespeare's *As You Like It* for English class and finds that he likes letting out the Rosalind in himself. Rob now encounters gender-bending issues in other parts of his life and struggles with identity issues as well as dating. A lighthearted young-adult novel.

Peters, Julie Anne. *Far from Xanadu*. New York: Little, Brown, 2005.

Mike (Margaret-Ann) Szabo, an atypical young woman pursuing her late father's plumbing business, struggles with identity issues in an accepting small Kansas town, not identifying herself as a lesbian but lusting after Xanadu, the hot new big-city arrival. A serious, engaging, and heartrending young-adult novel.

———. *Keeping You a Secret*. New York: Little, Brown, 2003.

In this beautifully heartwrenching love story, Holland Jaeger, a high school senior, surprises herself by falling for the school's visible lesbian, Cece Goddard. A young-adult novel that encourages readers of any sex or orientation to feel deeply as they experience a story whose outcome is not so unusual for queer teens.

———. *Luna*. New York: Little, Brown, 2004.

Regan narrates the story of her brother's transition from Liam to Luna and the reactions of family and community as the transformation occurs. An award-winning young-adult novel by a talented author.

Woolf, Virginia. *Orlando: A Biography*. New York: Harcourt, Brace, 1928.

A classic gender-bending tale spanning centuries, this love letter to Vita Sackville-West disguised as a fictitious biography follows the life of Orlando from his beginnings as a sixteenth-century nobleman to the novel's end, where Orlando becomes an early twentieth-century woman. A masterpiece of language and wit whose character transcends time and gender.

Magazines and Newspapers

Print

Most large cities have at least one LGBT newspaper this can usually be found distributed free of charge in the lobbies of gay-friendly businesses, or paid subscribers can have papers delivered directly to a mailing address. Other well-known periodicals are listed below.

The Advocate, a national biweekly magazine
 for the GLBT community
P.O. Box 311
Newburgh, NY 12551
www.advocate.com

*Bay Windows: Boston's Largest Gay
  & Lesbian Newspaper*, weekly
631 Tremont Street
Boston, MA 02118
www.baywindows.com

Chrysalis Quarterly, a quarterly publication of AEGIS
AEGIS
P.O. Box 33724
Decatur, GA 30033

Cross-Talk, a publication of the Northern Concord
Northern Concord—the U.K. Transvestite/Transsexual
  support group
P.O. Box 258
Manchester M60 1LN
United Kingdom
www.northernconcord.org.uk

*innewsweekly: New England's Largest Gay & Lesbian News
  & Entertainment Weekly*
450 Harrison Ave., Suite 414
Boston, MA 02118
www.innewsweekly.com

Transgender Tapestry, a quarterly publication of IFGE
International Foundation for Gender Education
P.O. Box 540229
Waltham, MA 02454
www.ifge.org

YGA magazine, published bimonthly by Young Gay America
3107 Isleville Street
Halifax, Nova Scotia
B3K 3X9 Canada
www.ygamag.com
www.younggayamerica.com

Online

advocate.com (www.advocate.com), the online version of
  The Advocate

inNewsweekly.com (www.innewsweekly.com),
  companion to the print *innewsweekly*

Oasis Magazine (www.oasismag.com)

365gay.com (www.365gay.com), a daily online news source
  for the LGBT community

Transgender Forum (www.tgforum.com), a weekly magazine

Glossary

HELPING PEOPLE UNDER-
STAND GENDER ISSUES
HELPS YOU, TOO

NSSEXUAL

NSGENDER

HAM

5-alpha-reductase pseudohermaphrodite a rare genetic disorder passed down within families where the person's external genitals are of normal size for females, but who also have Wolffian ducts and testes

ambiguous genitalia external genitals that are neither clearly male nor clearly female, but could be either, or both

Androgen Insensitivity Syndrome (AIS) a genetic condition that is the most common diagnosis of male pseudo-hermaphroditism[1]

Androgen Resistance Syndrome *See* Androgen Insensitivity Syndrome

androgynous; androgyny having the characteristics of both sexes; someone who appears both male and female at once

asexual sexless; not experiencing sexual attraction

berdache in some Native American cultures, a male who dresses and behaves in the role of a female; though *berdache* are respected members of their communities, the term was used derogatorily by European colonizers for Native persons who did not fit their expectations of gender (*see also* Two-Spirit)

binding *See* chest binding

biological sex a term used to classify one as male, female, or intersex based upon physical, genetic, biological, and hormonal characteristics, including genitalia

bisexual of or pertaining to two sexes; a person sexually attracted to both males and females

boi alternative spelling for *boy*, used mostly by alternative boys, FTM gender-benders

"bottom" surgery genital reconstruction as part of sexual reassignment surgery

brain sex the organizational structure of a person's brain, which is said to differ between male and female brains

breast augmentation surgical enlargement of the breast tissue

butch displaying masculine characteristics or appearing more masculine than feminine; generally used in conjunction with *lesbian*

chest binding tight wrapping of the chest area designed to flatten breasts, creating a more masculine appearance in the body

chromosomes biological structures in cell nuclei that carry genetic information; most humans have twenty-three pairs of chromosomes, with the standard female having two X chromosomes (XX) in the last pair and the standard male an X and a Y chromosome (XY)

circumcision removal of the foreskin of the penis, often done as a religious rite by Jews or Muslims

clitorectomy; clitoridectomy surgical removal of the clitoris

clitoroplasty plastic surgery on the clitoris

closeted hiding one's gender identity/expression or sexuality from public view and only sharing information deemed acceptable by society

congenital adrenal hyperplasia (CAH) the most common form of intersexuality, CAH is an inherited condition that causes the malfunction of the fetal adrenal gland resulting in an excess of androgen;[2] most CAH babies are assigned female and a majority develop a female gender identity[3]

cross-dresser a person of one physical sex (or gender) who dresses in the clothing of the opposite sex or gender

drag the clothing/attire of the opposite sex; to be *in drag* is to be dressed as a person of the opposite sex

drag king a woman dressed as a man, often a lesbian appearing/performing as a man

drag queen a man dressed to appear/perform as a woman

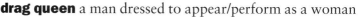

dyke derogatory term for a lesbian unless used by a member of the lesbian/gay community

epispadias a birth defect where the urethra exits on the upper side of the penis[4]

faggot derogatory term for a gay man unless used by a member of the lesbian/gay community

femme from *effeminate*; displaying feminine characteristics, often used in contrast with the word *butch*

FTM; ftm; FtM; F2M female-to-male transsexual; someone assigned a female gender at birth but who identifies with a male role

gay (slang) technically, a man whose sexual preference is for men, that is, a male homosexual; may be used to describe a lesbian (as in "a gay woman" or "she's gay")

gender one's sex; usually either male or female, but intersex does occur

gender ambiguity when one's gender is not easily discernable by others

gender attribution others' perception of one's gender

gender dysphoria (GD) psychiatric term used to describe a person who is unhappy with his or her gender role in society, specifically when one's *gender identity* differs from one's *gender*

gender expression the gender role one plays; the way one expresses gender through dress, movement, speech, and behavior (*see also* gender role)

gender fluid genderqueer

gender identity the gender with which one identifies internally, whether or not this matches the body's physical sex or genitalia

gender identity disorder (GID) psychiatric term used to describe a person who is unhappy with hir gender role in society, who feels greatly at odds with the gender ze was assigned at birth and the associated gender role expectations; currently a psychiatric disorder, just as gay and lesbian people were considered mentally ill into the 1970s

gendermap a term coined by Dr. John Money to refer to the entity, template, or schema within the mind and brain unity that codes masculinity, femininity, and androgyny[5]

gender noncomforming persons crossing the boundary lines of gender who may or may not consider themselves transgender

genderqueer; GenderQueer slang term for a person crossing the boundary lines of gender expression; often used by persons who may or may not be transgender, but who feel their gender falls outside of the male/female dichotomy

gender role the role one plays (or is expected to play) within society as dictated by gender-specific behaviors and one's gender assignment at birth

genital surgery surgery to change the appearance of one's genitals, as may be done when sex determination is made difficult by ambiguous genitalia; not to be confused with sexual reassignment surgery

genotype the genetic makeup of an organism

gestation the period of time when a fetus is developing in the uterus

GLBTQI gay/lesbian/bisexual/transgender/queer or questioning/intersex

gonad organ that produces gametes for sexual reproduction; in humans, testes and ovaries

gynecomastia abnormal enlargement of the breast tissue in males

HBIGDA the Harry Benjamin International Gender Dysphoria Association

heredity also called "nature"; that which is passed on through genes to offspring

hermaphrodite an outdated term for a person with both male and female sex characteristics, today called "intersex"; that the hermaphrodite could have full genitalia of both sexes is a myth, and the "true hermaphrodite," where both ovarian and testicular tissue are present, is exceedingly uncommon;[6] some find the term stigmatizing and misleading, and members of the intersex rights movement would have the term abandoned[7]

he-she a butch (masculine) lesbian; a person whose gender expression is male and whose birth sex is female

heterosexual a person (male or female) who is sexually attracted to persons of the opposite sex

hijras the people in India deemed "neither men nor women"

hir gender-neutral pronoun to replace *her* and *his*

homophobia an irrational fear of nonheterosexual persons

homosexual a person who is sexually attracted to another of the same gender

hormone therapy; hormone replacement therapy (HRT) the introduction of hormones to a body to treat a condition; for transgender individuals, HRT is employed specifically to develop characteristics of a gender other than the one assigned

hypospadias a birth defect where the urethra forms an opening on the underside of the penis[8]

hysterectomy surgical removal of female sex organs; removal of the uterus, at a minimum, and possibly also including removal of the cervix, ovaries, and vagina

intersex a person born with an anatomy or a physiology different from the cultural norm of male or female and who displays both male and female sex characteristics; sometimes erroneously called a hermaphrodite

ISNA Intersex Society of North America

karyotype blood test used to detect a chromosomal anomaly

Klinefelter Syndrome a common chromosomal variation in which males have an extra X chromosome (usually written as 47,XXY), which may cause sterility, breast development, and incomplete masculine body build; many Klinefelter Syndrome males lead such normal, healthy lives that they are never diagnosed

lesbian a woman who is sexually attracted to other women; a homosexual woman

LGBTQI lesbian/gay/bisexual/transgender/queer or questioning/intersex

mastectomy surgical removal of one or both breasts

Mayer-Rokitansky-Kuster-Hauser Syndrome (MRKH) a congenital variation in typical XX females, MRKH girls are born without a completely formed uterus, fallopian tubes, and/or vagina; the condition is also known as Congenital Total or Partial Absence of the Uterus or Vagina, Mullerian Agenesis, Vaginal Agenesis, and MRKHauser Syndrome

metaoidioplasty plastic surgery to enlarge the clitoris to resemble a penis

MTF; mtf; MtF; M2F male-to-female; someone whose assigned gender at birth was male but who identifies as female

nadle in Navajo culture, a person who plays a male role, including that of mediator between men and women

nature heredity, as used in reference to growth and development; natural, inborn characteristics that are unchanged by one's environment

nurture environment, as used in reference to growth and development; those aspects formed in response to one's living conditions and life experiences

omnisexual a person who is sexually attracted to persons of all genders

out visible to the public; to not be in hiding; also, to reveal another's undisclosed sexual orientation (from the phrase *out of the closet*)

packing slang for the insertion of an object into a person's pants in order to give the appearance of a penis

passing slang for being perceived as other than what one is (for example, a lesbian might pass as straight, or a transgender person may pass as being the gender ze desires)

phallic reconstruction the surgical re-creation of a (damaged) penis

phalloplasty plastic surgery on the penis or the building of a penis by plastic surgery

phallus penis

phenotype the observable makeup of an organism

phimosis a condition of the penis that prevents retraction of the foreskin

postoperative transsexual a transsexual who has had her or his body's physical structure surgically altered to have the genitals of the sex opposite from that with which ze was born

preoperative transsexual a transsexual planning or preparing to have his or her body's physical structure surgically altered to incorporate the genitals of the sex opposite from that with which ze was born

primary sex characteristics those determinants of sex present and observable at birth, including the external genitals and internal sexual parts

Progestin Induced Virilization a condition where an XX (female) baby has an enlarged clitoris and no testes; such a child is sometimes assigned a male identity and raised as a boy[9]

pseudohermaphroditism a condition whereby the chromosomal and external genital makeup of a person do not match; in male pseudohermaphroditism, which represents about one-third of the intersex population, the XY person has testes (usually undescended) and "female" genitals; in female pseudohermaphroditism, which also represents about a third of the intersex population, the XX person has ovaries and "male" genitals[10] (*see also* hermaphrodite)

queer strange or odd from a conventional viewpoint; unusually different; unconventional; slang for homosexual (*see also* genderqueer)

real-life experience (RLE); real-life test (RLT) period spent living full-time as the desired gender as a prerequisite to sexual reassignment surgery

secondary sex characteristics those determinants of sex that appear with puberty, including, for females, development of breasts and hips, a softer feminine physique, maturation of genitals, appearance of body hair, and the onset of menstruation; for males, development of a more masculine build, maturation of genitals, deepening voice, protrusion of the Adam's apple, and appearance of body hair

sex one's gender as determined by the presence (or absence) of gender-specific genitalia (*see also* biological sex)

sex reassignment; sexual reassignment surgery (SRS) surgery altering a person's body, specifically the genitalia or secondary sex characteristics, to that of another sex; sought to bring one's gender identity and one's body into alignment

she-he a drag queen; a person whose gender expression is female and birth sex is male

sie (pronounced "see") a gender-neutral pronoun to replace *she* and *he*; sie provides an alternate spelling and is synonymous with *ze* or *zee*

SOC acronym for Standards of Care; refers to the HBIGDA SOC established in 1977

SRY acronym for the *sex-determining region of the Y chromosome*

straight slang for heterosexual

Testicular Feminization (TFM) an outdated name for the genetic condition now called Androgen Insensitivity (or Resistance) Syndrome

TGNC transgender and/or gender nonconforming

"top" surgery breast reduction or augmentation as part of sexual reassignment surgery

tranny boy; tranny boi someone who identifies as a female-to-male transgender person; the spellings vary and may include hyphens or be written as a single word

transgender one who crosses the boundary of the gender expression assigned at birth; this person may choose to undergo sexual reassignment surgery and/or treatment with hormones; technically, any homosexual, but most do not identify as transgender

transition the period of change when a trans person begins to live more fully as a person of his or her true gender, possibly including a required period of full-time living before sexual reassignment surgery

transman; TransMan female-to-male transsexual or transgender person

transphobia irrational fear of persons whose gender does not fit within the binary system of male/female

transsexual one who crosses the boundary of the sex assigned at birth; he or she may or may not opt to undergo sexual reassignment surgery and/or treatment with hormones

transvestite a public cross-dresser; one who wears the clothing of the opposite sex and will appear before others dressed in this fashion, but who identifies with the gender corresponding to the gender expression assigned at birth

transwoman; TransWoman male-to-female transsexual or transgender person

trimester a period of three months, often used with reference to academic calendars or human gestation

Turner's Syndrome a condition describing females who carry the genetic code XO (rather than the standard XX); lacking ovaries, they demonstrate exaggeratedly female behavior accompanied by sterility

Two-Spirit Native American cultures allow for more than two genders and includes transgender people as Two-Spirit or two-soul people, also known as *berdache* or, in the Crow nation, *badé* (or *boté*); among the Maricopa, *kwiraxame'*; among the Chumash, *joya*; among the Cocopa, *warhameh*; or among the Zuni, *Ihamana*[11]

urethra the tube that extends from the bladder to the outside, through which urine passes and, in men, through which semen travels

urethroplasty surgical extension of the urethra, the result of which allows a person to urinate while standing up[12]

vaginectomy surgical removal of the vagina

vaginoplasty plastic surgery on the vagina, especially the building of a vagina by surgery

Wintke a common shortening of *Winyanktecha* or Two-Souled person, recognized as a third gender in parts of Native American culture

womyn; wimmin alternative spelling for *woman* or *women*, removing the male root of the word

ze; zee gender-neutral pronoun to replace *she* and *he* (*see also* sie)

NOTES

1. Suzanne J. Kessler, *Lessons from the Intersexed* (New Brunswick, N.J.: Rutgers University Press, 1998).

2. Kessler, *Lessons from the Intersexed*, 165–66.

3. Cheryl Chase, e-mail message to author, 23 May 2006.

4. "What Are Hypospadias & Epispadias?" in the Frequently Asked Questions of the Hypospadias and Epispadias Association (HEA) website, www.heainfo.org/shell_resources.htm.

5. Anne Vitale, "Gender Identity Disorder: A Brief Description of the Problem," in *Notes on Gender Transition*, rev. 2 April 1997, www.avitale.com/GID.html.

6. Kessler, *Lessons from the Intersexed*, 13–14.

7. Intersex Society of North America, "Is the Person Who Is Intersex a Hermaphrodite?" www.isna.org/faq/hermaphrodite.

8. "What Are Hypospadias & Epispadias?"

9. Intersex Society of North America, "Progestin Induced Virilization," www.isna.org/faq/conditions/progestin.

10. Kessler, *Lessons from the Intersexed*, 166–67.

11. Leslie Feinberg, *Transgender Warriors: Making History from Joan of Arc to Dennis Rodman* (Boston: Beacon Press, 1996), 23–25.

12. Mildred L. Brown and Chloe Ann Rounsley, *True Selves: Understanding Transsexualism . . . for Families, Friends, Coworkers, and Helping Professionals* (San Francisco: Jossey-Bass, 1996), 208.

Index

HELPING PEOPLE UNDER-
STAND GENDER ISSUES
HELPS YOU, TOO

NSSEXUAL

NSGENDER

HA...

About the Author and Illustrator

HELPING PEOPLE UNDER-
STAND GENDER ISSUES
HELPS YOU, TOO

NSSEXUAL

NSGENDER

HA

Cynthia Winfield graduated from Lesley College in 1992 with a bachelor of science degree in middle school education, and from Emerson College in 1999 with a master of fine arts degree in creative writing. A licensed educator in the state of Massachusetts, she enjoys teaching eighth-grade reading, writing, and language arts in a suburb of Boston. Her interest in quiet political activism—mostly around issues of equal rights, health care, literacy, and education—has brought her together with the gay community since the mid-1980s when she began volunteering for the AIDS Action Committee of Boston, then served as volunteer secretary for the McLean Association for Gay, Lesbian, and Bisexual Issues committee at McLean Hospital, in Belmont, Massachusetts. An active participant in Seeking Educational Equity and Diversity (SEED) seminars since 1999, she derives pleasure from her interactions with colleagues at her local SEED seminars, at New England SEED Leaders' seminars, and at gatherings of the national SEED program at the Wellesley College Center for Research on Women. Settled in the northwest suburbs of Boston with her family, she feels fortunate to lead a quiet life wherein she enjoys reviewing books for *VOYA: Voice of Youth Advocates* magazine and contemplating the earthy simplicity of vermiculture in her spare time.

Erin Lindsey has been creating comic strips since the tender age of nine, but is best known for her long-running transgender comic strip *Venus Envy*. An accomplished writer and illustrator, she has had the experience of living as a member of either sex, something she often tries to capture in her work. Twenty-five years old, Erin is studying animation and illustration at the Art Institute of Seattle. Her hobbies include rock climbing, baking, and reading other comics.